MAGICAL I
MAGICAL IMAGINATION

Third Edition

GARETH KNIGHT

SKYLIGHT PRESS

This expanded edition first published in Great Britain in 2012 by Skylight Press, 210 Brooklyn Road, Cheltenham, Glos GL51 8EA

Chapters 1-7 originally published in 1998 and 2003 by Sun Chalice Books, Oceanside, California.

Designed and typeset by Rebsie Fairholm
Publisher: Daniel Staniforth
Cover photo by Matt Baldwin-Ives

www.skylightpress.co.uk

Printed and bound in Great Britain by Lightning Source, Milton Keynes
Typeset in Adobe Caslon Pro. Titles set in TierraNueva Norte, with Swirlies.

British Library Cataloguing in Publication Data.
A catalogue record for this book is available from the British Library.

ISBN 978-1-908011-52-7

Contents

The Magical Imagination

WHAT IS a Magical Image? First we had better ask ourselves what we mean by magic.

As far as we are concerned it is a mental discipline for training certain aspects of our mind so that we can realise our full spiritual potential. So that we can develop a series of natural gifts that perhaps we never knew existed.

There is far more to each one of us than just a physical body. We have instincts and emotions, rational (and irrational) thoughts, and also a sense of moral responsibility. This complex of faculties is sometimes called the soul. And when our soul departs, at the end of physical life, the body decays. It reverts to the basic laws of its physical components when it is no longer a vehicle for soul expression.

Yet there is even more to the soul than what we have just defined. It has other dimensions, inner powers and perceptions that often escape our attention during physical life. We become so consumed with the process of 'getting and spending' that these inner powers, perceptions and soul dimensions may never be fully realised. Yet the existence of these higher powers can be proved by experience, given the proper training.

Our souls and bodies are the projection of a yet higher self, whose core is a divine spark of creative spirit. The aim of magical training, then, is to become aware of, and to use, this vast potential that lies within. We may then start to behave like human spiritual beings, rather than as a higher kind of animal.

When we extend the range of our perceptions beyond the world of the physical senses we become aware of an 'occult' or hidden world. It is called hidden, or 'occult', simply because it is not immediately obvious to our outer senses. Yet it is a perfectly natural world, it has always existed, and is made up of our own higher consciousness as spiritual beings. And also of the higher consciousness of the spiritual beings of others with whom we can communicate.

The way we can extend our awareness of these levels is by a process of 'tuning' consciousness. This is very close to the principle of radio. A vast range of radio waves exists all about us, morning, noon and night, and yet we are unaware of it. Although if we have a functioning radio receiver we can tune in to any wavelength we choose.

Now all of us carry within us a magical radio set. It is a perfectly normal human gift, yet because it is so rarely consciously and properly developed it tends to be classed as 'supernatural'. This engenders a certain amount of fear and superstition, which are both unnecessary attitudes. Our own inner powers are not of the devil, and nor are those who have developed them bizarrely gifted.

We all have psychic ability. It is our birth right, and it can be trained and developed, just like any other normal skill, be it reading or writing, singing or dancing, playing the violin or swinging from a trapeze. Some people will of course have slightly more or less basic ability than others, but whatever natural talent we have can be cultivated. And we can develop our range of skills to fit our personal needs and aspirations.

We learn to 'tune' consciousness by various forms of meditation, and for the most part this is a training of the imagination. When we do this our imagination ceases to be just an interior picture show of subjective fantasies. It becomes a means of perception. It forms an 'inner eye' and 'inner ear', and vehicle for other 'inner' senses that give us knowledge of the 'inner' worlds. And although we may call them 'inner', this does not mean that they are only subjective. There is more to the magical universe than mere psychology.

We are accustomed to take the imagination somewhat for granted, even to denigrate it. For many people it seems to be no more than a vehicle for wish fulfilment fantasies, or a subjective refuge for those who seek escape from the 'real world'. Yet the worlds available through the higher use of the imagination are every bit as real as the physical world.

Indeed we would not be conscious of our existence in the physical world without the power of imagination. And so it will be helpful if we look at the faculty of the imagination a little more closely. It can be usefully divided into three specific functions, under a nomenclature devised by an early pioneer in these matters, the romantic poet and philosopher, Samuel Taylor Coleridge.

The first function of it we may call the **Fancy**, and this is the usual conception of the imagination, as an interior picture show that associates and recombines images that have come to us from the external world. It enables us to manipulate and fashion new ideas in a visual way, whether the medium of expression is a mathematical theorem or a surrealist painting. It is the basis for original and creative thought, how new things get invented, how stories are told, pictures painted, plans made. In other words, it is the stage for the whole process of interior reflection, practically applied.

There is another form of the imagination however, that is equally or even more important, even though we tend to take it for granted or ignore its existence. This is the interpretation into meaningful structures of the raw impressions that come to us, as stimuli to our physical senses, from the physical world.

If a blind man suddenly receives the gift of sight, it is some time before he is able to interpret that sudden blast of light impressions. He has to learn to reconstruct this kaleidoscopic barrage into a series of pictures that make sense. This is an ability that most of us learned in early childhood, to translate sense impressions into a system of representations that we can regard as an ordered world about us.

This unconscious or automatic organising of sense data is the work of a type of imagination that is so basic and fundamental to our process of physical awareness, that we can appropriately call it the **Primary Imagination**.

There is another form of imagination however, and one equally difficult to detect unless we know what to look for. It is the type of imagination that interprets the impressions that come to us from the higher worlds.

It tends to work in powerful images and so is particularly appropriate to religious experience and to the arts. These images are generally called symbols, because as well as being images in their own right, they may also stand for something else, something 'other' than themselves. They 'resonate' with other meanings. They have a certain power or numinous quality about them. This is apparent in the significance we feel about the imagery of certain dreams.

We do not have to be in dream consciousness for this type of imagination to work, however. It is to be found wherever a certain fascination is felt about any particular image.

This can be the charisma about a certain person, be they lover or leader, or about a special object, be it religious relic or souvenir of past times. It may be felt in a profoundly moving piece of prose or poetry or drama, or before any great work of art. It can also be associated with places, pilgrim shrines or sites of scenic grandeur. Something is being represented beyond the surface reality and meaning of the object itself. All this is the province of the **Secondary Imagination**.

The Secondary Imagination works largely through the agency of symbols. There are various grades of symbol, the simplest of which are purely intellectual ciphers, such as mathematical, scientific or other conventional signs that are used as a form of convenient shorthand to represent certain physical quantities, objects or processes. The symbols, however, that we wish to designate as magical images are those that do not merely *represent* something else. A magical image *resonates* to a higher kind of reality. It carries within itself something that is 'not of this world'.

By systematic work upon these magical images, in all their rich variety, we may become aware of our own higher selves and the greater world of which they form a part.

Magical images themselves have different powers and purposes, and we can divide them into certain types. One division is between animate and inanimate images, which in turn can be further divided. Animate images may be human or non-human. Inanimate images may be simple objects or complex structures (see table).

Inanimate magical images form a natural sequence rather like a series of chinese boxes, one within the other. That is to say, we may start by finding our bearings by means of a cosmic chart or map; this leads us to going on a journey through an inner landscape. We may then make our way as pilgrims towards a particular temple or other sacred structure. In this we may find a shrine, wherein may be certain numinous objects.

Animate			Inanimate	
Human	Non-human		Objects	Structures
teachers	animals		numinous artefacts	cosmic maps
ancestors	angels		abstract symbols	landscapes
historical	elementals		pictures	temples
fictional	extra terrestrials			shrines
gods				

There is a similar hierarchy of *animate magical images* although in not quite so clear cut a sequence. Small animals, sometimes in the form of 'totem animals' may lead us on part of the way. Figures of elemental beings or angels, of various grades, commonly act as guardians or guides to further levels. Any instruction received is likely to come from contacts with human forms, be they spiritual teachers or guides, or personal ancestors, relatives or more widely known historical figures. More exotic contacts can take the form of anything from ancient god forms to visitors from outer space, or may take on the characteristics of well known fictional or legendary characters. Indeed, any form may be encountered, which the human imagination is capable of visualising and using as a means of inspiration or helpful guidance.

Unpleasant images are liable to induce unpleasant experiences but such are likely to occur only in negative circumstances. Such circumstances include debased motives in pursuing this kind of study, for 'like attracts like' in the dynamics of the inner worlds, which implicitly calls for high moral standards in any intending magical practitioner.

Nervous sensitivity or over-impressionability is another negative condition, that may be a simple lack of spiritual will, social responsibility, or self respect, possibly exacerbated by ill administered hypnosis or the influence of drugs.

If any imaginative figure appears unacceptable, for whatever reason, it can be made to transform to more congenial form. We are, after all, unless neurotic or pathological, masters of our own interior theatre. It is our own creative imagination that we are using as a magic mirror and we should be well able to control how it responds to inner or outer stimuli.

If, for whatever reason, we cannot so control it, then magical study and practice is best left alone, at least temporarily. The cure for most psychic problems lies not in exorcisms or protective talismans, which tend simply to feed the self-induced delusions by granting them importance and reality, but in grounding our attention and faculties into things of the physical world. Thus the best antidote to any problems of an over-stimulated imagination is a good meal, a hot drink, and diverting company or entertainment; or for those of a more Spartan turn of mind, hard mental and physical activity and a cold shower!

Most contacts and images, let it be said, being of the higher worlds, will be constructive, beauteous and healing. We are, after all, seeking and dealing with symbols of growth and enlightenment. Let those who seek baser goals think seriously about who or what they may be contacting, and what the motives of their intended play-mates are likely to be.

What we meet when we persist with good intent in magical work is, however, genuine friendship and guidance from inner levels that help us with the living of life in a rewarding and constructive manner. The path is not without its challenges, but the forces we contact will be working within the remit of divine intelligence, and so all progress will be that of spiritual growth. Heavier challenges may be vouchsafed us at a more advanced level of our studies, but we shall by then be well able to cope with them, and no one is pushed beyond their capabilities.

The means by which such instruction will come to us is through a whole range of magical imagery, so we will examine each type of magical image in turn, to see what type of guidance and instruction we are likely to receive from it.

Cosmic Charts and Maps

COSMIC CHARTS or maps are not so much magical images in themselves as systems of magical images. They are means whereby individual symbols or magical images may be inter-related. With their help we can see the general outline of where we are at, whence we have come, and where we are going.

One of the most important of these cosmic schemes is shown in Figure 1. Here we see the Earth placed at the centre of the universe. The Earth itself is made up of the traditional elements of Earth and Water, surrounded by an envelope of Air, beyond which is a sphere of Fire. Then come the Heavens, which are in the form of a series of crystalline spheres, each one associated with one of heavenly bodies visible to the naked eye, that appear to pursue a wandering path through the sky. Their order is Moon, Mercury, Venus, Sun, Mars, Jupiter and Saturn.

Beyond these seven spheres is one that contains the fixed stars. These include not only those that make up the twelve constellations whose magical images are the signs of the zodiac, but a further thirty-six, for there were forty-eight constellations recognised by astronomers of the ancient world to have a symbolic or magical resonance. (The other constellations listed today are comparatively modern additions, based upon the intellectual fancy of seventeenth or eighteenth century astronomers, and not the fruit of the all important Secondary Imagination).

A tenth crystalline sphere beyond all the others is known as the Primum Mobile and is regarded as the sphere of the angels. Traditionally there are nine orders of angels but the ones particularly associated with the Primum Mobile are those who cause all the crystalline spheres to turn. These angels are thus the prime movers of all life and action in the universe.

Figure 1: The Crystalline Spheres

And beyond this great construct of crystalline spheres, surrounding all, is the Empyreum. This is a state of being beyond all the Heavens which is the source of them all, the Fount of Creation.

Most of this great system of imagery comes down to us from the ancient Greek philosopher Aristotle, who collected together many of the scientific and philosophical ideas of his time. Much of it was lost when the Roman empire fell to the barbarian hordes, but it was later restored by medieval scholars, and in particular by St. Thomas Aquinas.

There was some resistance to this at the time, because some conservative theologians, particularly at the University of Paris, deemed it pagan knowledge, not sanctioned by Biblical authority. Nonetheless it was largely accepted as a useful system and served as the framework of one of the greatest works of world literature, Dante's *Divine Comedy*.

It came in for further criticism in Renaissance times, when it began to be realised that this system of imagery was not a true representation of the physical universe. Thus in 1543 the mathematician Copernicus tried placing the Sun at the centre of our planetary system, and later scientific astronomical observation confirmed his theory to be true, despite strong rearguard action by church authorities, as in their celebrated attempt to muzzle Galileo.

This completely exploded the old Aristotelian system as a valid description of the physical universe, but what the ecclesiastical reactionaries and their successors the modern materialists failed to realise, is that it remains a very useful description of the spiritual and praeter-natural universe of which the physical universe is but a shell.

For in magical and spiritual terms, not only the Earth, but each individual upon it, is a centre of the universe. And this is because each individual perspective of the universe is unique and as valid as any other. Thus, from the collective standpoint of humanity, the Earth remains at the centre of the system. So when it comes to experience of the inner worlds, the old system still holds good, and provides channels of imagery through which psychic and spiritual force will flow.

We do not have to accept this as a dogmatic principle, for we can try it out for ourselves. Let us use it as our first practical example of the use of magical imagery. And although we cannot guarantee results or instant success for everybody, the exercise we give has proved effective for a number of students of widely differing backgrounds.

Invocation of the Spheres

Be still within your room and form a dedicated centre. If there is a group of you, sit in a circle around a candle or sanctuary light. If you are alone, or if there are only two or three of you, imagine you form part of a circle of like-minded souls who seek to aid you in your work. It does not matter if you do not recognise your invisible co-workers. Simply be aware of them in faith.

Be conscious of the world of nature outside your room: of the trees, the plants, the flowers, the small animals, and the elemental beings that organise their forces. Be aware, if you will, of the great being of the Earth, Gaea herself, within her body of earth and sea.

Be aware of her breathing, of the air enclosing the surface of the Earth; the movement of the winds across the landscapes and the oceans; the rise of water into the air through the warmth of the Sun, and its precipitation again as dew, rain or snow. See the clouds in the skies as changing expressions upon the face of nature.

And at the limits of the atmosphere see an encircling sphere of protective light. This has sometimes been called a ring of inner fire. It is the spiritual counterpart of what is called the ozone layer. It withholds and protects the beings of the Earth in many unsuspected ways.

Now imagine a sphere of crystal whose extent about the Earth is as high as the Moon. You may imagine the figure of the Moon upon its sphere, if you will, but there is no need to visualise more. Simply be aware that the crystal sphere itself represents the tuned consciousness of an order of angels that beams down strength and constancy to humankind and all that live and move and have their being upon the planet.

There is no need to dwell long in this realisation once the initial effort is made. Extend your visualising powers to another crystal sphere whose bounds extend to the distance of Mercury. Be aware of this as the focused consciousness of angels of intelligence and communication, bringing intellectual light to the denizens of the Earth below.

Now extend your vision to another crystal sphere, one that coincides with the orbit of Venus. It represents and radiates love and beauty to all below.

Pass on to visualise a further sphere, this one radiant with the Sun's light and as high as the Sun. It beams down, like the rays of the Sun, health, harmony, light and life-giving power to the Earth within its care.

Next see a crystalline sphere that coincides with the orbit of Mars, the focus of angelic beings of truth and right and justice.

Beyond this one, visualise the sphere that corresponds to the orbit of Jupiter and mediates the angelic influence of order and benign rulership.

And then imagine the crystal sphere that has at its limits far-off Saturn, and mediates the principles of organisation in form and the upholding of the necessary laws of nature.

Beyond this sphere is one that has engraved upon it, as on a crystal decanter, all the stars of the heavens visible to the human eye from Earth. These are the star angels whose influences pour in from the constellations. Not only those of the zodiac but of the other great asterisms such as the Pleiades and the Great Bear, and brilliant individual stars such as Sirius, Polaris, Regulus, or Vega, that beam down a plethora of spiritual influences that are necessary for the well-being of the Earth.

And then beyond this is the outermost sphere of all, of complete clarity. It is the sphere of the holy angels themselves, sometimes called the Primum Mobile, that keeps all the cycles of being moving, be they cycles of time or cycles of space, of birth and growth and death, of individuals or of nations. And if you listen carefully, you may hear the angels singing; it is what has sometimes been called the harmony of the spheres – not only the harmony of the working of a beautiful organism, but also a paeon of praise for the Creative Spirit beyond who conceived it.

Our consciousness is not capable of penetrating beyond the outer sphere, even in symbolic vision. But a reflection of what lies beyond can come to our awareness. As an expression in sight and substance of the harmony of the spheres, see a holy rain begin to fall. It is as delicate as newly forming dew, like the lightest of light mists. And it falls gently but inexorably through all the spheres. See it pass through each and every one until it falls upon the Earth outside your room and brings a freshness and a new-washed feeling to all that is within.

And as you become aware of this you may see, in your midst, at the centre of your circle (which is also the centre of all the crystal spheres, and whose ultimate circumference is beyond them all in the Uncreate Reality), a growing radiance.

You may see, or be otherwise aware of, no more than a sense of love and light, although many have seen standing in the centre a child, the Son of Light, the Ever-living Young One, radiating peace and seeking personal and individual contact with each and every one, head to head, heart to heart, and feet to feet, as signifying the Way.

If you can, be aware of and reciprocate this contact, and seek to mediate it to the world, so that it penetrates all humanity, and influences the actions of your own small life. Now let the vision fade, and return your attention back to the world of your present duties and desires.

This spherical model of the universe of magical images is capable of considerable elaboration. Dante filled his vision with a vast range of ancillary symbolism, including contemporary political events and personalities which, unless we are scholars of fourteenth century Italian history and culture, are not too helpful to most of us today. Nonetheless this great work of medieval literature is an interesting example of how a general Cosmic Chart or Plan can be broken down into various landscapes, which is the next stage for the practical use of magical imagery.

For instance Dante's cosmic traveller starts in a dark forest, aware of fearsome beasts that may be a threat to him, as he tries to make his way towards a green hill in the distance. This turns out to be the start of a very long journey, for after meeting his guide, the poet magician Virgil, he is led on a path down into the Earth and through a series of underworld scenarios that are a reverse pattern of the heavens that we have just described. Passing through the centre of the Earth he comes, on the other side of the world, to a mountain whose spiral ascent leads through various ordeals of purgation and tests to the Earthly paradise – the Garden of Eden before the Fall. From there, with the assistance of his ideal lover Beatrice and other heavenly guides, he rises through each of the Crystalline Spheres, meeting their angelic and other denizens, until he emerges into the Empyreum. Here there floats a great white rose, the *rosa mystica*, each of whose petals is made up of spiritual beings, and whose golden centre is the throne of the Godhead. Dante's *Divine Comedy* was therefore not only a work of literature but a chart for the examination, cure and ascent of the soul in spiritual self realisation.

Nor was it the last use of it in this manner. The most well known illustration of the system, and arguably the best, is the famous engraving by De Bruy for the seventeenth century Rosicrucian Robert Fludd, showing the Soul of the World as link between God and Nature.

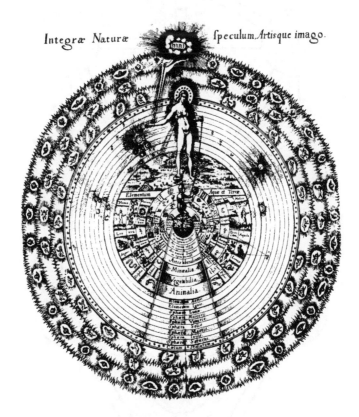

Figure 2: The Soul of the World as a link between God and Nature

There are, however, many other ways of depicting these dynamics, and one of the most useful is the Tree of Life of the Qabalah. This is also a series of circles, although not usually set out one within the other, but laid out in a pattern of triangles and squares. That is, there is a network of 'paths' connecting the spheres, as in Figure 3.

At first sight this may not look much like a tree, but essentially it is a pattern of relationships, and in this sense it is akin to a family tree. However, the inter-relationships are not of social alliances

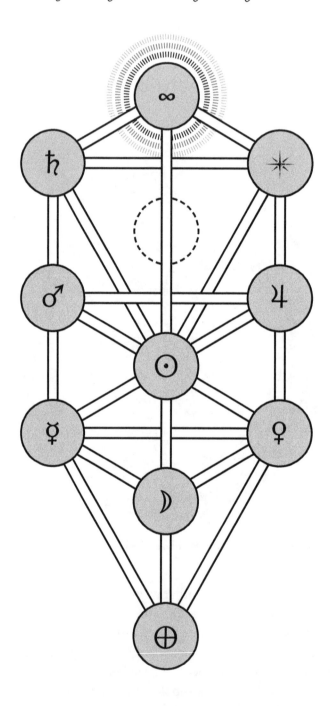

Figure 3: The Spheres of the Tree of Life

but the dynamics that go to make up the structure of any created being. In other words it is a *general systems model* of the principles of creation.

Each circle on the Tree corresponds to one of the crystalline spheres in our previous diagram, and they are in the same order. That is, starting at the top and zig-zagging down – in a sequence that is known as the Lightning Flash – they represent the Primum Mobile, the Fixed Stars, Saturn, Jupiter, Mars, the Sun, Venus, Mercury, the Moon and the Earth. There are also three Veils beyond the Primum Mobile and indeed surrounding the whole Tree, that represent the outer aspects of the Empyreum.

The benefit of the pattern of paths between the spheres is that they can themselves be invested with symbolism or magical images, and we can pass by them from one sphere to another, in visualisation. The Tree of Life has thus become a major tool of meditational training in the West because it enables us to inter-relate a vast compendium of magical images and associated experience.

Each sphere, for example, can be imagined as a temple building, with each path as a journey through a symbolic landscape between them. We shall come to examples of symbolic landscapes later. For the moment it is sufficient to realise that the Tree of Life is a Cosmic Map that enables us to tap into many types and levels of experience, for each circle is not only a crystalline sphere with planetary attributions. It can readily carry a whole host of other applications.

As an illustration of this we can try some practical work with magical images based upon the Tree of Life applied to the aura, although first we will need to say something briefly about the aura that surrounds each and every one of us.

As well as a physical body we each have more subtle vehicles for our soul to indwell. At its lowest level we can think of this in terms of a kind of electromagnetic cloud that extends a certain way into physical space all around us. This is our personal 'atmosphere', although it has more subtle elements to it than the psycho-physical or the electromagnetic. In its subtler aspects it extends a considerable way into what we may come to know as 'inner space', and these are of considerable potential power.

We can visualise the aura in various ways, but the simplest is in terms of an ovoid shape, becoming more sphere-like as it extends. It then becomes not unlike the system of crystalline spheres we have been describing, and these spheres have links to different psychological dynamics within us.

Looked at in another way, however, the aura can also be seen to contain a system of power points, and these power points have a certain correspondence with the system of spheres on the Tree of Life.

Remember in all of this, however, that we are dealing with the powers of the imagination, and formulating *magical images*. There is no direct link between the images we shall be building and the endocrine glands, or the psycho-physical power points within the etheric vehicle that are known in the East as the *chakras*.

This is, in one sense, a safety mechanism, for it is possible in advanced yoga techniques, with the aid of certain postures and complex breathing techniques, to work with visualisations and chants that impinge directly upon the etheric body and the autonomic nervous system. This may well be a valid mode of progress for those who can emulate the conditions of an oriental contemplative monk, including close supervision by a personal guru and rigid conditions of diet, life style and seclusion.

The western methods we advocate do not aim permanently to sensitise the inner faculties but rather to arouse these powers for a specific short space of time only. This is the prime purpose of group meditation and ceremonial actions or ritual. Here, the play acting or dramatic faculty is used to heighten the secondary imagination by the controlled use of symbolic story lines. We can do the same thing by the individual visualisation and intelligent use of magical images.

This being clearly understood, we can start to build up a framework of personal magical images based loosely upon the cosmic charts of Crystalline Spheres and Tree of Life, and these can be usefully and safely related to the dynamics of our own aura.

First let us take into account the basic polarity of spirit and matter. Within the make-up of man this is represented by the Divine Spark and the Physical Body. In terms of magical images within the aura each can be seen as a power point visualised as a disc of light. One just above the head, which represents our individual spiritual principle. The other just beneath our feet, which represents the pattern of our life on Earth.

Midway between these two points, on the physical level, we have a muscular wall within our torso, called the diaphragm. This plays a major role in our breathing, in the essential process that keeps our body functioning from minute to minute. The diaphragm, although a physical organ, represents an important inner division within our aura.

Above it are the heart and the lungs, concerned with the intake and expulsion of life giving air, and the circulation round the body of its carrier, the blood. Below it is a massive nervous centre called the solar plexus, and the stomach and other organs concerned with the intake and processing of food to fuel the fires of the body.

We can now formulate the basic spiritual and material poles within our aura, and an operational mid-point between them.

A disc of diamond light above our head, which represents the fount of our spiritual integrity; that spark of divinity, or divine impress, which makes each one of us unique as an individual human being.

Another disc beneath our feet, which we can imagine ourselves standing upon, or which our feet rest upon if we choose to take up the other best position for practising western meditation, a poised sitting position with the spine straight, and the hands resting upon the tops of the thighs, which are horizontal with the ground, with the assistance of a small foot stool if necessary.

This disc can be seen in the traditional colours of Earth, which are four-fold. Quarters of citrine, olive, russet and black, the type of colours often associated with the autumn, or which colour the skin of certain apples. This represents our earthly expression. Our fate, our destiny, our path through life, and how well integrated we are with the physical world about us.

Between the two, as a kind of large circular breastplate, we can visualise the mid-point disk like a great sun of gold. This combines two auric centres. The heart, which is associated with our higher ideals, our aspirations, our feelings of personal vocation or destiny. And the solar plexus, which links us in fellow feeling with others, either in personal friendship or emotional ties with family or loved ones, and in a more general sense, of team spirit, loyalty or other types of enthusiasm.

There are two further discs we may now take into account. Two centres of creative expression.

The higher one we can visualise before the throat as a lavender coloured disc. The throat contains the organ of speech, that which above all distinguishes us as creative and highly communicative beings above the level of the 'dumb beasts'.

The lower creative centre we share with all the animal creation, and it is represented by a deep purple disc before our organs of generation, which above all physical characteristics differentiate us in gender, and the fount not only of biological creativity but of the libidinous drive that lies behind much physical action and ambition.

We have now formed the five spheres of what, on the Tree of Life, are sometimes collectively called the Middle Pillar. This nomenclature implies of course that there are other pillars, and we can also formulate the spheres for these, one to each side. We shall meet the Pillars again when we come to consider the magical imagery of the temple or shrine, but they have a place here in helping us to formulate a Cosmic Map against the background of the human aura.

We can visualise the two side pillars to our right hand and left hand, sufficiently wide apart for us comfortably to stand between them. The one to our right we may call the Dark or the Black Pillar, and the one to our left the Bright or the Silver Pillar, although there are various other names for them. They represent the ever present duality of any possible expression we can make, the positive and negative aspects of any action or decision, the active or passive attitude we may adopt and so on, whatever functions are conceived as opposite or complementary poles of each other.

So much for the general principles of building the Tree of Life within the aura, the overall pattern for which is shown in Figure 4. We will now pursue it as an individual exercise, the regular performance of which should soon give proof of its beneficial value.

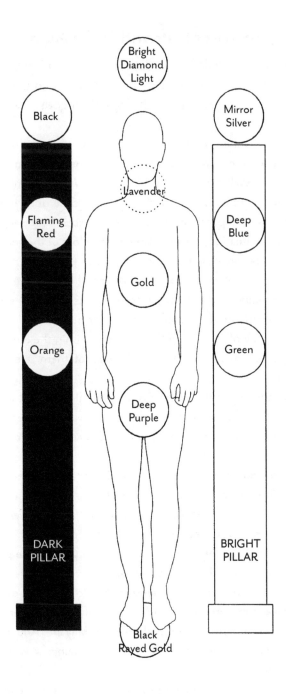

Figure 4: The Tree of Life in the Aura

Building the Tree of Life within the Aura

This exercise is best done standing, in a relaxed but poised attitude, or in the seated position already described, which is not unlike that found in certain depictions of the Egyptian gods.

Steady your breathing by becoming conscious of it, and be aware of the in-breath taking the same amount of time as the out-breath, with a similar pause between each inhalation and exhalation. A slow mental count of four can be a useful guide to begin with. This should be done in as normal and comfortable way as possible; do not breath excessively deeply as this may lead to hyperventilation, causing dizziness and loss of the gentle self-control of your faculties that we are seeking.

Now be aware of a point of bright diamond light above your head. You may, after a while, physically begin to feel it, as an actual sensitivity at the top of your scalp, but do not strive unduly for this. Each of us as individuals has our own way of registering these centres within the auric envelope and secondary phenomena like this, or the lack of them, are not necessarily indicators of progress.

This 'becoming aware' of your own spiritual point just above the head, (rather after the fashion of a personal halo), is a valuable exercise just in itself, and can be usefully and harmlessly practised at any time of day in convenient circumstances.

Now turn your attention to a point just beneath your feet, as if you were standing upon a disc. You can visualise this as if it were a golden maltese cross upon a black ground. Again you may find a certain very slight tingling sensation beneath your feet when you have performed this for some little time. This is a natural feeling of etheric sensitivity that some people may get, and once again, should not be consciously striven for. It is a minor natural effect, not a supernatural phenomenon to be blown up out of all proportion.

The real and important effect of building of these two centres in the aura should be in grounding you spiritually in your daily life. And in one sense it is a kind of wordless prayer to your own spiritual being, or your holy guardian angel if you like.

You can take your time over this, building up just the two points before you go on to construct any more of the Tree in your aura. One step at a time will bring more effective and lasting results. But when you feel ready you can pass to the next stage, which is to visualise a great golden disc, like the sun, over your diaphragm, so that if it were physical, it would be like a circular breastplate, covering your lower chest and upper abdomen.

You may feel quite a warm glow of love and well-being from this exercise. And as you grow more accustomed to it you can try to feel and to separate out those feelings which seem to pertain more to your heart, that is above the diaphragm, and those which pertain more to the solar plexus, just below the diaphragm.

In esoteric terms you will be beginning to differentiate between two of the Spiritual Alchemical Elements – that of Air above the diaphragm, and that of Water below. This has its physical correspondences in that above the diaphragm we have the lungs, the organs of breath, and below the diaphragm and digestive organs with their largely liquid related functions. It follows that the centre above the head corresponds to the Alchemical Element of Fire, (Spiritual Fire and the Divine Spark), and that below the feet to Alchemical Earth. When we have all four in balanced function we are on the way to expressing the Quintessence, which is our full human capability, greater than the sum of its parts.

Having well established this centre of our being we can pass to the remaining two centres, and you can build these two together, for they relate closely to one another in function, although at different levels. You can formulate them as slightly smaller discs than the golden central one. A disk of a beautiful lavender colour, just before your throat; that is, at the topmost point of your torso. And a similar disk of a deep purple before your generative organs, before the lowermost point of your torso. You may find it helpful to elaborate this symbolism slightly by seeing a silver star in the higher lavender disc, and a crescent moon, (points up), in a purple sky in the lower.

We have now formulated the Sephiroth of the Middle Pillar of the Tree of Life within the aura, and the benefits of this should soon become evident in greater poise and inner equilibrium. To this may be added the side Pillars. You may best visualise these as if you were standing between them. See and 'feel' a dark pillar to your right and a bright pillar to your left. This should give a further sense of well grounded balance and stability. Upon each pillar you can then imagine, when you are ready, three further discs.

It may be best to build these in pairs, at any rate in the first instance. At a level with your head, be aware in the right hand pillar of a dark, almost black sphere, and upon the left hand pillar one of bright silver, almost like a mirror.

These represent quite high intuitive or mental functions of which you may not hitherto have been very aware within yourself. But this form of visualisation will in the course of time start to bring this kind of awareness about, in the form of flashes of intuition or inspiration or clear-sightedness.

It is not easy to make an intellectual definition of the difference between these two topmost pillar points, because their functions are above that of our normal intellectual consciousness. It must suffice to say that the silver is like the intuitive receptivity to the highest spiritual wisdom, and the black is like a dark womb of understanding, particularly of the application of uncreate realities into the restriction of form-expression and consciousness. More, we cannot usefully say at this point.

At the next level, corresponding more or less to shoulder height, you can become aware of two discs representing two sides of yourself, that might be summed up as what you are and what you do. On your right side see therefore a disc of flaming reds, that indicates yourself in action, going and getting and doing. And balancing this upon your left side, a disc of deep blue that indicates yourself in calmness and wisdom taking full account of your own strengths and weaknesses and the needs and demands of the moment before embarking upon any action. You can, given sufficient practice, utilise these two discs quite actively in daily life. Concentrating upon the red one when action and initiative are called for, and the blue one when you need to hold back and assess a situation carefully before committing yourself to an action you might later regret.

Finally, we come to the discs at about hip level upon the side pillars. To the right you can build an orange disc which represents the right control of your mind and intellect, and to the left, one of green that represents right expression of your emotions. Again, concentration upon these when you need to use your wits when facing an intellectual problem, or to keep the right level of expression or control in an emotional situation, are practical applications of this particular exercise.

We have now examined and gained some practical experience of a couple of Cosmic Maps or Charts. There are, it should be said, a number of others from which we could have chosen. In the East, for example, apart from the detailed yoga practices, a similar all inclusive system is to be found in the imagery of Mount Meru. This is a fabulous island which compromises the whole universe, with its hells of hungry ghosts and assorted demons below, and upon its peak a city of the gods and above that a series of heavens; whilst all around is a great ocean with mighty islands and an all encompassing ring of cosmic mountains.

Other, more abstract systems exist, such as the Enneagram; a system of nine points round a circle, which has a mathematical basis and derives from Sufi mysticism. It is much favoured by followers of the spiritual teachers Gurdjieff and Ouspensky and has also been developed as a psycho-therapeutic device by some groups within the Roman Catholic church.

However, it does not serve our purpose to make a comprehensive collection of systems, which would call for a work of encyclopaedic proportions, and only increase our intellectual knowledge rather than our wisdom and understanding. The ability to work confidently in one or two systems is of more use and benefit than a superficial knowledge of many.

And although some of these systems may appear to differ quite fundamentally in their outer appearance, they do have an underlying unity. This is because they are describing the same basic principles but are simply using a different symbolic language, or system of magical images, to do so.

Landscapes and Journeys

WHATEVER COSMIC MAP we choose will help us to understand how the inner world is structured. In this sense a Cosmic Map is a comprehensive magical image in its own right. If we identify with it and build it as a pattern within our own aura it helps us to maintain personal balance and gain general understanding of our own spiritual potential.

However, it will also reveal more if we examine and experience it in its detailed parts. By moving from one part of the system to another, we will find ourselves embarking upon a quest, or initiatory journey. The overall cosmic map becomes therefore a ground plan for a number of possible journeys through ordered states of consciousness.

In practical terms, any journey must take place through some kind of landscape. So the next stage of our practical work with magical images is to use them in a linear way that will take us through an initiatory journey or story.

Such journeys are common in all myth and legend. There are stories of adventure, of quests, of pilgrimage, of exploration, of rescue, of conquest. Any story has some kind of initiatory potential. That is what makes story-telling so popular throughout the ages. Some stories may have more numinous content than others but even the most banal tale can have its resonances with deeper journeyings within and beyond the soul.

We have already mentioned Dante and his long journey through the underworld to a mountain of purification and his subsequent ascent into the heavens. This is an example of a Cosmic Map being used quite directly as a system of landscapes for visionary travel.

However a multitude of others exists. Some are plainly allegorical and piously explicit, as Bunyan's *Pilgrim's Progress*. Others may be scatological and hilarious adventures, as Apuleius' *The Golden Ass*, which conceals some of the mysteries of the Graeco-Roman cult of Isis. The ancient Greeks had their quest of the Golden Fleece by a band of heroes. And in later times an amalgam of Celtic mythology, British prehistory and Cistercian and Near Eastern mysticism provides us with the Arthurian knights and their various quests including that of the Holy Grail.

These mythological and legendary sources tend to be quite compendious and too long drawn out for practical use in their entirety. Although their value as stories to be read and contemplated at leisure is by no means diminished.

What we seek in our process of 'tuning consciousness' is, however, something a little more specific than the whole sweep of an epic or volume of tales. And there is nothing to stop us selecting the bits that we need from the vast rich treasure store of myth, legend and religious tradition.

Whatever the source or background of the magical journeys we choose to make, there are various key scenarios that are particularly apt to the tuning of consciousness. We may list a few examples:

a) a desert journey towards a temple in the wilderness;
b) a pilgrimage along an ancient track toward a sacred circle or mound;
c) a boat journey down a river to a sacred city or island;
d) a sea voyage to a mysterious island or sacred shore;
e) an underground passage to chambers deep within the earth;
f) the ascent of a winding stairway in a mysterious tower to a chapel or watchtower;
g) an aerial journey by chariot and flying horse or other means to a temple in the sky or among the stars.

The detail can be taken from any existing fictional or historical writings, adapted to choice, the main criterion being the evocative stimulation of the imagination. Accomplished and imaginative practitioners will be able to write their own, either prepared in advance for reading, or extemporaneously expressed at the time of working. However, as beginners, we are likely to need the support of external sources and preparation.

In its basic and most elementary format, the tuning of consciousness through an imaginary journey may be used as a preparation for magical work. In this function it is commonly called a *Composition of Mood* or *Composition of Place*. In fact the imagery of the imagined place induces the required mood (an elementary pre-tuning of consciousness onto more or less the right wavelength), and in turn the induced mood aids in forming subsequent spontaneous imagery.

Let us take an example. In order to cover as many aspects as possible within a short compass we will make it a journey that leads from the temple of our own being, into an inner objective world that is experienced first as an ancient trackway through open country, that leads to a tower in which inner objective states may be experienced at various levels.

We will choose a symbolic landscape that is likely to appeal to a majority of students, the traditional countryside of old England around Glastonbury, broadly associated with the Arthurian and Holy Grail legends.

Composition of Mood: The Path to the Tower

Being seated comfortably in your meditation position, free from likelihood of disturbance, calm and compose yourself with a minute or two of regular relaxed breathing, and proceed with the formulation of light within the aura as described in the previous chapter.

Now open your inner eyes to the realm of creative visualisation, and feel yourself standing upon a disk quartered in the traditional colours of the Earth: citrine, olive, russet and black, which slowly disappears as you find that you are standing upon a hill top in open countryside. A light breeze fans your face, the warmth of the sun high in the heavens is upon your body. Hear the bird song in the trees and hedges, and smell the scent of spring flowers. Beneath your feet is a rough trackway, its natural chalk surface rutted with the passage of flocks and herds and horse and cart traffic through the centuries. And also of pilgrims, for this is an ancient trackway across the Land of Logres, the legendary country of King Arthur, Merlin, the Lady of the Lake, the Grail Castle, and many another sacred and ancient mystery.

The track takes a wandering course across the hills and along with your companions of the way, you follow this ancient way of pilgrimage. It is a pilgrimage towards the holiest earth in Logres, to Glastonbury, the meeting point of many sacred traditions, some of them older than recorded time, some even older than time itself.

The trackway leads over the last of the hills, a long, low mound that is like a sleeping beast, and is called by the locals Wearyall. Upon its furthest slope you pause to stand beside a thorn tree. This is by tradition the holy thorn where Joseph of Arimathea planted his staff which then miraculously blossomed. To the west can be seen the glint of waves on the distant sea, across the salt marshes. But your eyes are turned across the valley that lies before you, of monastic buildings, and villagers' huts of wattle and daub, to two hills upon the opposite side. One is the emerald green round swell of Chalice Hill, at whose foot lies a holy well. And rising high beside it the pyramid-like shape of Glastonbury Tor, with a spiral path around it leading up to a lone tower.

You pass swiftly down the side of Wearyall Hill and through the low lying ground that lies between until you reach the foot of the Tor. Here you scramble up a short steep path to reach the foot of the spiral way. Beside a stile where the spiral path commences, you find a figure gowned in white, a guardian of the Tor, one of the Watchers of Avalon, who has guarded, loved and prayed in this place over the long ages.

This little journey will suffice us for the moment. We can usefully break off here without becoming committed further. And we will take up our journey again a little later.

We have effectively conducted a short Composition of Mood, or Composition of Place, in which we have tuned our consciousness to a particular wavelength or inner dynamic. We can now either proceed or withdraw consciousness back to the physical world. This can be done by retracing our steps in imagination back to the place whence we started and return by that route to our own hearth and home. Such a return procedure need not be long drawn out. Some people prefer to unwind more quickly or more slowly from inner consciousness, and retracing the path, either slowly or at speed, is an effective way of doing this.

However, it is also possible to return to outer consciousness more quickly still, simply by affirming the will to do so. And indeed in the (hopefully rare) case of physical interruption of a meditation, this may be a necessity. This can be a bit of a shock however, particularly if we are deeply into inner consciousness, or if we are of a more sensitive than average disposition. But apart from this minor discomfort there is no need to feel open to dangers about letting inner forces into your outer consciousness in an uncontrolled fashion. There is much needless fear about this, or of the dangers of getting 'stuck' if one does not meticulously retrace every step of the way. This is a result of taking the sensible precautions often built in to elementary training procedures a little too seriously. It is always better of course to err on the side of caution but this does not mean that we have to have two belts and three pairs of braces to hold our trousers up.

Having been spiritually centred to begin with in your visualisation, after the manner we have described, you are always in control. And even if pulled back suddenly from a very deep inner experience you can always affirm the proper boundary between worlds by means of a simple ritual gesture, such as stamping your foot or clapping your hands, or making a sign of closing curtains, followed by a warm drink or light snack. This is perfectly adequate for any person of normal balance and sensitivity. There is no need to be the psychic equivalent of James Thurber's aunt who worried about electricity leaking into the house if there were no electric light bulb in the socket. Once you have switched off your mental radio receiver you will not continue to hear the programme.

Let us take stock of what we have actually been doing. We have started on an imaginative journey that consists of visualising, in linear sequence, a selection of numinous symbols or magical images.

We began by stimulating our spiritual consciousness and psychic and intuitive sensitivity by a simple exercise of channelling light within the aura. This done, we evoked a pleasant country scene, with an ambience of ancient traditions and aspirations to quest or pilgrimage. This slowly crystallised into a specific location, which in this case was Glastonbury Tor, which is a sacred site of some power in its own right, with both pagan and Christian associations.

It helps to use sites of this type, particularly if you have had the opportunity to visit them physically at some time in the past. A previous visit not only sharpens up your visualising ability with regard to that particular place, but also forms a subtle etheric link with part of your own aura. This can be more effective than performing rites or meditations at the actual physical site, where satisfactory conditions and freedom from interruption can seldom be guaranteed. In other words, it can prove more effective to make the etheric link with a simple visit, as any tourist, and then to re-evoke the inner dynamics in the controlled conditions of your own temple or own home.

You can also take liberties with an inner landscape and improve slightly upon nature, which is a time honoured method in any branch of art. Thus we commenced the journey upon a real ancient trackway, the Ridgeway, which although in physical fact passes a number of ancient sites such as the Uffington White Horse and the Avebury megalithic complex, is not geographically associated with Glastonbury. However, its inner resonances are those of any ancient trackway, and could be readily utilised in this instance.

However, it is not essential to have actually visited any of these physical sites to perform effective work. They can indeed be entirely fictional. The main criterion is that they move us emotionally, in however slight a way. It is that slight movement of emotion that provides the initial power for our working with the images. It is a form of priming the pump. Later, as our work progresses, the images will begin to feed back a power of their own. We then have 'lift off'.

And so let us now resume our journey. Having broken off it may be best for you to start again at the very beginning and work your way through to the point we have reached. For those with a little more experience in these matters it may be possible effectively to take up immediately where we left off. There is no such thing as an outer time lapse upon the inner planes. However, remember in all of this that as in all acquirement of a natural skill, it is better to 'make haste slowly.' In other words, do not skimp on the five finger exercises if you really want eventually to play the magical keyboard well.

In the continued journey that follows we shall find that there can be journeys through interior locations as well as through landscapes, and also that we may meet with figures of people or other beings on the way. For the moment we will simply take these as they come, without too much dalliance, until we have gained some experience of dealing with inanimate magical images. The more complex issues surrounding our possible relationship with animate images will find their place later.

The Journey to the Tower (continued)

For the moment we simply take note of the Watcher of Avalon who stands at the start of the spiral path that leads up and around the Tor.

We clamber over the stile, assisted by the robed figure, who at the same time takes the opportunity to scrutinise us deeply with a penetrating gaze.

Once over, we start up the steep track, worn in the chalk, that takes us up in a clockwise direction around the conical hill. We are aware, as we climb, of the strength of elemental life about us, in the grass and wild flowers, cropped by the grazing cattle through which we pass. We are conscious of the sweep of the Somerset levels as we pass ever higher upward, marshes that some short while ago were under the sea, when the Tor and its surrounding hills were islands, and now cut with the straight gleaming lines of 'rhines' or drainage ditches.

Finally, somewhat breathless, we arrive at the top of the Tor, and there standing before us is a tower. However, it is not the bare and broken down tower that is visible upon the physical plane, the remains of a demolished church, but an altogether grander edifice, an inner tower known only to those with the power of vision.

The door to the tower is set high up above the ground. This signifies that none who are unworthy are allowed to enter in, but by virtue of our dedication we find we are expected, and a wooden ramp materialises in the air, leading from before our feet to the door itself. And feeling an ambience of welcome from the invisible guardians, we are allowed to pass across.

Our feet ring hollowly upon the boards, and at the top, at the narrow wooden doorway, we are greeted by a fair maiden, who, with many willing hands to help her, takes our travel-stained outer clothes, and places us at our ease.

The large circular room is warm and bright. An open fire roars in a great fireplace against the wall before us. The atmosphere is one of a welcoming home, with love and peace and gentleness pervading all. It is here we may also meet with friends from outer life, or of loved ones, be they in or out of physical life. For this is the place of the centre of the heart's desire, the true hearth of every home, and its fire is the central fire for every family hearth. We may refresh ourselves within its atmosphere and take some essence of it back to our own homes in the outer world when we depart. The maiden, who is the tender of the hearth, tells you that you will always be made welcome here.

We are also conscious, after a while, of levels of the tower that lie beneath us. And as we start to think about this a door bursts open, and standing within the portal is a great strong man, in appearance like a blacksmith. He has curling chestnut coloured hair and rippling muscles and smiles broadly. He wears a leather apron and bears the hammer and tongs of a smith. We see that he stands at the top of a stairway leading downwards, and he beckons and invites us to see what is there.

We descend a spiral stair that is as narrow and tightly turning as that within a mill, and as we reach the bottom we pass into another warm and welcoming room. We find we are standing on a rough stone and earthen floor. The whole place is like a cellar, lit with a ruddy glow from fires, some of which heat an oven, from whence there comes the fragrant smell of new-baked bread. There are also stills against other parts of the walls, some fermenting wine and other strange liquors and herbal essences.

We can see that animals are stalled here, for there are secret gates that lead out through the hillside to their pasturage. We also see the sleek coats of horses, along with the duller coats of cattle in to be milked. In another part of the cellar stands a blacksmith's forge and anvil for the making of tools and weapons. There also appears to be a kiln for making pottery. The mighty smith looks on all around him with pride and is pleased that we are impressed with the diversity of his crafts.

Then he places his finger to his lips, and points to a dark corner we had not noticed before, and we see that he is indicating a trap door set in the floor. We look at it, wondering where it might lead, and as we do so, become aware of a figure who moves forward from the shadows beyond it.

He is an old man, with a long white beard, holding a staff. Suddenly he produces from beneath his dark grey cloak a lighted lantern, which he fixes to the top of his staff. Then, with surprising agility, he bends forward and throws open the trap door.

We see a flight of rough stone steps leading downwards into the earth. With a glint in his eye that could be either of warning or of humour, he raises his lantern aloft, and proceeds down the stairway, indicating that we should follow.

We pass down a dark and steeply descending stairway, conscious only of the bare earth ceiling and walls about us, and the dim light going before, ever downward. We also feel that we are observed, but by whom or what we cannot imagine.

At last the downward journey ends, and we find ourselves in an underground cavern. As our eyes grow accustomed to the dark, lit only by the old man's lantern, we see that we are in a crypt. On ledges and crevices in small ante-chambers and passageways are coffins. But there is no atmosphere of decay or death or neglect, but rather of a living ancient wisdom, as of memories and dreams from remote ages. We feel a sense of kinship with all that is held within this place. We are in the presence of a sort of sleeping treasure house of human experience.

This is the place of the ancestors. Our own ancestors, of our own blood line or of other races who have inhabited the land of our birth.

We are conscious of the sound of the flowing of underground waters. And by listening to this soft background murmur we find it can be a vehicle to tune in to the thoughts and dreams of those who have gone before on life's way. Whose lands we share and inherit, or through whose veins there ran the same blood that courses through our own. And from this place we can receive love, strength and advice of an enduring and earthly wise nature. Here is the source of all family and national tradition; in stories, rhymes, myths and legends. We rest here awhile so that we may recall this ambience when, in times of stress in the outer world, we need the wisdom and strength of the past.

Now the old man indicates that it is time for us to depart, and looking toward the stairway, we find that we have been joined by another guide. This one is also one of our forebears, and yet he also has another guise and function, for he is one of the greater guides and guardians, who helps to guide the destinies and well being of nations. He has a Tudor style of dress, a scholar's cap of that era, and a golden chain around his neck, of linked S-shaped devices, from which depends a great seal of office.

He warmly greets us personally, holding our two hands clasped together within his own, before he leads us out of this place. After a salutation of respect and regard for its ancient guardian, he leads us swiftly up the stone stairway, back into the cellars of the tower, where the great smith stands holding a huge tray full of steaming fresh baked loaves, one of which we can take if we desire. We are also conscious, as we pass through this place, of fleeting figures, dimly seen, who belong here but are not of the human kind. They are elemental creatures of the green wood, of field and grove, river and lake, and as we realise their presence the smell of the loam and fragrance of the hedgerow and herb and wild flower comes also to our perception.

But we have no time to linger, for the master passes on, up the next spiral stairway, to the room that first we entered. It is full of friendly chatter and laughter and no cross words can be heard. We notice that from the windows can be seen an idyllic countryside. It is the ideal of the Land of Logres, the natural form of the Earthly Paradise as it could be expressed in the mode of the countryside of the Isles of Albion.

Again this is a suitable point where we can pause on our inner journey, in order to review some of the things we have seen and experienced. We have effectively made a small round trip and if we wish we can return the way we came, out of the tower, and down the Tor and along the ancient track to our starting point – or more directly if we so prefer, for the actual tower has its location within ourselves. What we have been doing, in effect, is to approach our own aura objectively from the outside (in imaginative terms), rather than subjectively from the inside.

When we went into the welcoming ambience of the room of the hearth fire it was as if we were becoming objectively conscious of our own solar plexus centre. We have made an objective place of it and have gone inside. Most of our journeys are thus within ourselves. Within our greater selves that is to say. Within the large ovoid of our aura that stretches all around us into inner space.

And when we then descended the stairs, first into the cellar under the hospitality of the blacksmith, and then into the caverns yet further below, under the invitation and the guidance of the hermit, we were experiencing something of the roots of our own being. These are represented by the lower psychic centres within the aura, corresponding roughly to Yesod and Malkuth upon the Tree of Life, in Qabalistic terms, the welcoming room above having its equivalent in Tiphareth.

It may come as a surprise that in search of spiritual values we should go down rather than up in our journeying through the tower. There are very good reasons for this, and we should also bear in mind that when we started our exercises of light within the aura we commenced at the top, at the crown above the head, and carried the light and the force downwards until it was at our feet.

From here we set out on our magical journey. And on this journey we have simply raised awareness up to the Tiphareth/Solar Plexus level again, when we entered the tower. And this enabled us the better to stabilise and go down to experience the lower dynamics, which normally are beneath the threshold of outer consciousness. This is a visit to the subconscious, or the unconscious if you like, should you prefer to use the more familiar (if implicitly materialist and limiting) definitions of analytical psychology.

Furthermore, it is very important to realise that we need to come to terms with these 'lower' dynamics, for they are as important, spiritually, as any 'higher' aspirations. The spiritual quest is not a flight from the problems and conditions of the physical world and our roots within it. It is one that seeks understanding and control of this lower world in which we live and move and have our being.

We are in no fit state to seek direct contact with higher spiritual forces if we have failed to come to terms with them in their expression in everyday life. To seek the higher whilst neglecting the call and the just dues of the lower, is to risk becoming that vague kind of subjective visionary who is out of touch with the practicalities of life and ineffectual in all mundane things.

We have, however, now taken a short magical journey, using images of an interior as well as an exterior landscape, which we have seen it is possible to interpret as part of a Cosmic Map. That is to say, in terms of journeys on the Tree of Life, up and down the central paths between Tiphareth and Malkuth, the central and the lowest spheres respectively. There is, needless to say, a lot more to the dynamics of what we have seen than this, but we have at least scratched the surface. Further experience building on from this will teach more.

However, we can now pass on to the next type of magical image, which consists of temples, shrines and the artefacts to be found within them.

Temples and Shrines

THERE IS GREAT variety in the structure of temples and all that goes within them. This includes the dedicated shrines that may form part of the edifice, and the consecrated or symbolic objects to be found there. However every magical temple conforms to the basic underlying pattern of an inner reality, just as every suit of clothes, however stylishly cut, must conform to the basic shape of the human form.

A magical temple is a model of the inner universe at large. Therefore somewhere or somehow within it there is likely to be a representation of the principle of duality. This is not the duality of good and of evil but the opposite poles of polarity (positive/negative, active/passive, force/form, light/dark, hot/cold) between which the web of life is strung. This is often found in the form of twin pillars, sometimes with an over-riding arch, and may be at the door of the temple or at some prominent place within.

There may also be a formal representation of the fourfold principle of the Elements that go to make up the substance of life. These are traditional states of being known as Fire, Air, Water and Earth. At the most physical and obvious level these universal principles are expressed in the four states of matter: plasma, gas, liquid and solid, but there is much more to the Elements than this. They embody basic qualities of expression at every level of manifestation, from the highest spiritual realms to the physical states of matter we have just described.

When expressed at the highest spiritual level they often appear in ancient symbolic forms. Examples from the Bible are the Holy Living Creatures of the Vision of Ezekiel, of Lion, Eagle, Man and Bull, which Christians later applied to the four Evangelists. However, they may be also seen, in slightly varied form, in the signs of the zodiac, the so-called 'fixed' signs of Leo (Fire), Scorpio (Water), Aquarius (Air) and Taurus, (Earth); or in the temple statuary of ancient Assyria, the winged lions, winged serpents, winged men and winged bulls.

These are, therefore, magical images of a particularly ancient and powerful type. However, before we embark upon the complexity of varieties of symbol let us see how the basic principles of duality and the quaternio can be expressed in the simplest possible way. This will be in terms of space. Or how the dedicated space of the temple is laid out. And as they are universal principles they will found to be latent in even the simplest plan.

The basic space could be imagined in the form of a square (or in three dimensions, a cube), conforming to our fourfold Elemental principles, one to each side, plus an overriding duality of Above and Below at ceiling and floor. But the simplest fundamental form will be a circle, or in three dimensional space, a sphere.

A circle, or a sphere, affirms by its very shape the principle of duality. As a first expression of Unity it has its single source or centre, from which every point upon its circumference or surface is equidistant. The primal duality is demonstrated in the complementary principles of the centre and the circumference. The centre is the focus of centrifugal force, and circumference is the expression of centripetal force.

We may now introduce the Elemental principles by the process of 'squaring the circle'. That is, we envisage a power point in each of the cardinal directions. So our temple may have an Elemental shrine at East and South and West and North.

It is traditional to divide these into temporal modes, according to the daily and yearly passage of the Sun in northern temperate zones.

Thus **East** is associated with Dawn and with the Spring;
South is associated with Noon and with Summer;
West is associated with Dusk and with Autumn;
North is associated with Midnight and with Winter.

The more esoteric Elemental attributions to the quarters are Air to East; Fire to South; Water to West and Earth to North. And these in turn are associated with traditional 'magical weapons', which have their correspondence in the suits of the Tarot pack, and even in the ordinary decks of modern playing cards that derive from them.

Thus East and the Air and the beginnings of things, represented by Dawn and Spring, is associated with the Dagger of Air in the magician's symbolic equipment. This has various adaptations, from the athame of the followers of Wicca to the sword of the ceremonial magician. Magic was practised by all ranks of medieval society and the difference between witch's dagger and magician's sword is essentially a social and economic one, between villein's cottage and baronial hall. An alternative might be any bladed instrument, and indeed the arrow head, as well as the knife that could be thrown, is particularly appropriate for dedication to Air.

In the South, associated with high Summer and with noon, we have the principle of Fire and this is adequately represented by the symbol of the rod or magic wand. Again this can come in various forms from the royal sceptre to the broom or staff of the country man or woman. There are some who feel that the sword is more appropriately associated with fire, largely on account of the familiar bellicose quotation of putting something to the fire and the sword, but the rod is the time honoured means of controlling and even of carrying fire. We use a rod or poker to control the domestic hearth fire or the celebratory or garden bonfire, and the god Prometheus is said to have brought fire to Earth within a hollow reed – another form of rod.

In the West, associated with evening, and gathering in of the fruits of the Earth, we have an appropriate symbol in the receptacle. This again can take many forms: as a chalice, as a drinking horn, and in the communal and culinary form of a cauldron. In the Arthurian legends it may be represented by the Holy Grail, which in fact has no well defined form, appearing in many guises in many situations but always bringing food and drink in material or spiritual form, and the renewal of life. A cup being principally formed to hold a liquid, the appropriate Elemental attribution is Water.

Finally in the North we may have an 'earthing' symbol. That which in some way makes sense of the past, confirms the physical present, and contains a plan for the future. This can be in the form of an orb, representing the Earth itself, or the Cosmos or a model of the temple as a whole. It can also appear as some kind of talisman, perhaps a disc of metal inscribed with a sigil of the dedication of the temple, or may be a simple dish containing an offering, and an earthenware dish is as appropriate to the Element of Earth as is one of costly gold or silver.

In the Centre of all we may place our centre of attention when the four Elements are in balanced equilibrium, that is to say an altar. The simpler this is, probably the better, for it represents the immediate focus of attention, and upon its uncluttered surface can then be placed whatever symbols may be appropriate to the work in hand. However, it is not uncommon, and entirely appropriate, to have some kind of unifying symbol associated with it. And most often this will be a light, sometimes hanging above the surface of the altar, whilst within its recesses may be kept holy relics or dedicated scripts that encapsulate the aspirations of those who use the temple.

From this basic outline very considerable complexity can be laid on. A simple but fruitful form of temple could be elaborated in terms of Tarot images, with the suits of Swords, Wands, Cups and Coins at the four quarters, with the Trumps ready to manifest at the centre.

The possibilities are legion, and in the end the personal temple of the magician, if working alone, reflects his or her own understanding of the inner universe. It is a personal three-dimensional Jungian mandala, should one choose to put it in psychological terms. And if it is a temple constructed by a group then it equally expresses the group's aspirations, or at least those of its founders.

To demonstrate some of the principles we have outlined, we can continue our journey through the tower. We do not have to retrace all the steps we have taken into the lower parts of the tower, but on entering the initial room of welcome can go straight up by the spiral stair to the level of the Temple of the Elements – led by our Guide to the higher regions, a man in the Tudor scholar's cap and golden chain of office.

The Temple of the Elements

We proceed up the spiral stairway, which has become quite wide at the top and gives on to a door. The door appears to be of cedar or of some similar resinous wood, and there is emblazoned upon it a five pointed star, point upward. This is a sigil that signifies the Spirit of man in control of and in cohesion with the four Elements.

Our guide knocks upon the door, three measured raps, and the door swings open before us. We are met by a waft of incense, which immediately raises our spirits to the work in hand as we push aside the heavy veil that hangs within the doorway, and pass within.

We find that we have come into a circular room, carpeted with a chequered design of black and white squares, indicative of the basic polarity behind all manifestations of life. Within the centre is a small altar, emblematic of unity, upon which there is a single light, upon a candlestick that is in the form of the caduceus of Mercury: that is to say with the two serpents of alternating polarity curled about its slender stem, and a pair of wings just below the flame. The altar itself is a double cube, that is to say, one cube placed upon another, which symbolically represents a figure of ten sides, the number that symbolically represents the Earth. There is a white cloth upon the altar, upon which rests an open book, its illuminated pages shining in the candle's light.

We see that there are four great circular objects at four quarters of the temple, that might well be huge windows, each concealed behind a curtain. That in the East is citrine yellow; that in the South is russet red, that in the West is olive green, and that in the North is black. Each is flanked by two pillars: the right hand one, as we look at it, silver, the left hand one gold. The tops of the pillars are spherical, the one on the left representing a globe of the earth, with its seas and continents, the one on the right representing the celestial sphere, with its constellations as seen from the earth. Arching above the pillars and joining their tops of the pillars is the sculpted form of an angel with outstretched wings above and hands upon the spheres. The name of each angel is written on a flying riband carved just below them. In the East Raphael, the angel of healing. In the South Michael, the protective warrior angel who stands in the sun. In the West Gabriel, the divine messenger. And in the North Auriel (sometimes called Uriel), the angel of light, the light of the stars of the night sky.

The door through which we have entered is no longer to be seen, being behind the ring of golden curtains, but our Guide stands there as guardian to mark its place. There is sufficient light from the central candle for us to see all clearly. And in the ceiling above the altar is another sculpted angelic form, whose wings spread widely above us, along with a riband containing his name, Sandalphon, the presiding angel over this temple of the Earth and of the Four Elements.

In that which follows, visualise yourself as doing the actions described – not as if you are standing outside yourself as an observer, but as if you are within your own body performing what is described. As a preliminary, imagine the feel of ceremonial robes about you. An inner robe of white, representing purity of intention, secured by a girdle of three stranded rope, one strand of purple, one of orange and one of green, that signifies the need for a threefold approach to the Mysteries of Earth, one of mystical devotion, one of magical knowledge, and one of elemental power.

Upon your feet are red shoes, representing the power to walk upon the higher planes. Upon your breast, pendant from a cord of golden ribbon about your neck, is a silver talisman, a disc that bears upon it a motto, chosen by yourself, representing your aspiration in your pursuit of higher knowledge and power. About your shoulders is a rich and heavy outer robe of gold, and upon your head a crown, that consists of a light golden band about your brow set with twelve gems, representing the signs of the zodiac, and at the apex of four arcs of gold arching up, a diamond above the crown of your head.

Now go to stand in imagination immediately at the western side of the central altar, facing eastward, and perform what is known as the Qabalistic Cross. That is to say, trace out in the air, with your right hand, first of all a point above your head, looking up towards the hovering angel above as you do so; and then sweep your hand and arm down to indicate a spot beneath your feet, feeling as you do so, the power of the presiding angel of the temple striking down into the earth below, and empowering with potential divine power the whole of the temple. Bring your hand back to your heart and then complete a form of the cross first to the right and then to the left, in an invocation of the powers of the pillars of equilibrium before clasping your hands before your heart and the sigil with your name of aspiration that hangs between your hands and your heart.

After a pause to take all this in, proceed slowly to the eastern quarter of the temple, before the citrine yellow curtains. Make the sign of a pentagram in the air before you, starting at the top, being conscious of the quarter's angel, towards which you point, and invoking his power and blessing as you do so, then swing your pointing hand down to lower left, up to upper right, straight across to upper left, down to lower right, and then back up to the top again. You may now intone the name of the angel Raphael physically if you wish (pronounced *Rah-phah-el*). When intoning in this manner physically, take a deep breath, and expel the air slowly by an upward movement of the diaphragm, letting the sound resonate in your head cavities as you do so. Relaxation is the key to success in this matter of 'vibrating' divine names.

Now, standing before the two pillars, imagine yourself taking hold of the centre of the curtains that hang between them, sweeping them back with an outward movement of your arms and step forward to stand immediately between the pillars of the east. You can, if you wish, vibrate the Qabalistic Holy Name of God associated with this quarter, as you stand there. This is the four letters of the name IHVH, pronounced *Yohd-Heh-Vow-Heh*.

As soon as you open the curtains, a bright light shines upon you and into the temple from the circular window before you, and you see that you are gazing into a landscape on an early morning in Spring, with the sun just rising above the horizon before you. Be aware of the singing of the dawn chorus of birds and of the diamond and rainbow scintillations of the dew upon the grass that begins to evaporate in the first beams of the morning sun. Although some remain to outline with crystalline brilliance the occasional spider's web, the drops are like the crystallisation of the worlds at the dawn of creation.

See just before the window a low altar upon which is a small dagger in a richly embroidered sheath. Take this up and draw the dagger, retaining the sheath in your other hand. Hold the dagger pointing upward and outward before you as if pointing to far goals or horizons, and hold the sheath, whose sigils contain the wisdom on how to use the dagger of spiritual initiative, immediately before your heart.

As you stand there, a large triangle of golden light begins to appear in the window space before you, point upwards, and with a golden bar across its centre, parallel to its base. This is the Triangle of Air. You then see a figure building in the air at each one of its points, outside the space of the triangle. At the topmost point is the figure of a handsome man or god holding a pitcher of water which he is pouring down all round the triangle, as if these were the waters of life with which he is fertilising a garden. Now see at the bottom left corner two children appear, like twin brother and sister, dancing in a fairy ring in the grass before a low wall behind which flowers blossom, rather like the Tarot Trump of the Sun. Then in the lower right hand corner of the triangle see the figure of a young woman build, throned and blindfolded and holding a sword in one hand, and prominently before her in the other a pair of scales, its pans swinging in equilibrium from the knife edge balance point; again similar to the Trump of Justice in the Tarot.

These figures at the three corners of the triangle of air represent the zodiacal signs of Aquarius, Gemini and Libra, respectively. Now, within the space of the triangle itself, see the figures of a faery king and a faery queen appear in the air, and dancing in the breezes all about them the whirling figures of sylphs, the traditional elemental creatures of air. You may vibrate the traditional name of their ruler – Paralda – to see them immediately burst into a dance of even greater activity.

You may stand contemplating this scene for as long as you wish. Then, in your own time, sheath the dagger and place it back upon the low altar before you, when the triangle and its figures will begin to fade. Then with the imagined or physically stated formula, "In the name of Yod – Heh – Vau – Heh, Raphael and Paralda I close the gates of the East," step backward a pace and draw the curtains between the pillars closed.

Go back to the central altar, and this time with your back to the east and facing west, perform the Qabalistic Cross, giving due intention of respect and thanksgiving to Sandalphon and go towards the Guide who stands at the door to lead you from this temple back down the spiral stairs.

It is probably enough that you devote the evocation of just one elemental quarter of the temple to each visit, although you should maintain a balanced routine by visiting each quarter in turn. The following instructions apply to the southern, western and northern quarters on subsequent visits.

For the southern quarter, having performed the opening Qabalistic Cross at the central altar standing on the northern side of it and facing south, proceed toward the russet red curtains, and in making the sign of the pentagram vibrate the angelic name Michael – pronounced *Mee-kah-el*. Open the curtains between the pillars with the Holy Name of Adonai – pronounced *Ah-doh-nah-ee*.

This time you will find that the warm and bright light of the noon day sun shines in upon you and that you are gazing upon a summer landscape with growth burgeoning throughout it in the trees and grasses and flowers, with bees humming from hives gathering in the nectar of the blossoms along with the coloured fluttering flight of butterflies.

Upon the low altar that stands before the window you will find a short magic wand, of hazel wood carved into a form of intertwining strands about a central shaft and bearing a dark tetrahedral stone at each end; that is to say a pyramidal figure of four triangular sides. Take up the wand and hold it immediately before you, and with your hand that holds its centre before your throat, you will find that its lower end is before your heart and the upper end at your brow. At the same time the lower stone of the wand glows with a dark green emerald light and the upper end a brilliant purple amethyst.

As before, a triangle begins to appear before you in the window, only this time without a bar across its centre. This is the Triangle of Fire. A figure begins to form at each point. This time at the top is the head of a lion, fierce and roaring at first, which slowly transforms into the figure of a young maiden leading it docilely with a chain made out of flowers, rather after the fashion of the Tarot Trump known as Strength. At the bottom left hand corner of the triangle there appears a centaur who holds a bow and arrow which he points upwards to fire over a rainbow. And at the bottom right the figure of a ram, looking round behind it as if to lead its flock, with golden fleece. These have their zodiacal equivalents in the astrological signs of Leo, Sagittarius and Aries.

Now, within the triangle, see the figures of a fiery masculine and feminine figure, the rulers of the salamanders, transforming creatures of fire, that writhe like lizards within the glow of a furnace and yet give an impression of power and wisdom, as if pictures of great wisdom and empowerment might be seen in their fire, which is as the heart of the sun. You may here vibrate the name of their ruler – Djinn – to see greater activity within their movement and possibly greater revelation within their fires.

When you are ready, return the wand to the altar, where its stones will cease to glow and the visions begin to fade. On closing the russet curtains do so with the formula "In the name of Adonai, Michael and Djinn I close the gates of the South". Then return to the centre and close as before.

For evocation of the powers of the western quarter, you start at the eastern side of the central altar, facing west, and perform the Qabalistic Cross before moving to the olive green curtains between the western pillars. The angelic name here is Gabriel, pronounced *Gah-bree-el*, and the traditional Divine Name AHIH, or Eheieh, pronounced *Ay-hay-ay*.

As you open the curtains you will find the light emanates from the sun setting in glory over the horizon of the western sea, but as if seen from upstream of a river estuary whereby you can see fields and orchards at the time of harvest home, at the season of mists and mellow fruitfulness.

Upon the low altar before the window will be a silver cup containing wine, the fruit of the vine, and you may raise this before you and visualise yourself drinking from the cup in salutation to the setting sun and in thanks for the fruits of the earth. Then, as you stand with the cup held before you, see appearing through the window before you, with the sea for its background, the Triangle of Water. This is a plain equilateral triangle that has its point downward. At the downward point you will see appear the form of a lobster or crayfish, the marine form of the astrological sign of Scorpio, the scorpion, that holds its claws out and upward before it in a way reminiscent of the balances of the scales of justice, and its tail curled up slightly at the end. To the upper right you will see a couple of fishes swimming in a circle, one silver and one gold, whose movement suggests a vortex of polarity similar to the oriental *taigetu* sign. And to the upper left see the form of a crab, of the hermit variety, that emerges from a spiral shell. These figures represent the water signs of Scorpio, Pisces and Cancer respectively. Within the triangle, stimulated into activity as you vibrate the name of their ruler, Nixsa, you can see a crowned mermaid and merman surrounded by water nymphs, or undines, in various forms and surrounded by various sea creatures of evocative shapes, such as sea horses, star fish or sea anemones, some of them perhaps bearing undersea pearls or other treasures.

Close this vision in a similar way to the others, by returning the cup to the small altar, and closing the curtains, to the accompaniment of the spoken formula: "In the name of Eheieh, Gabriel and Nixsa I close the gates of the west."

The ceremonial form for opening the northern quarter follows the pattern that has gone before. Commence at the southern side of the central altar, facing north. When you go to the dark curtains of the north, do so in the divine name of AGLA, an acrostic formula that means "Thou art mighty for ever, O Lord" and is pronounced *Ah-Glah*, whilst the relevant archangel is Uriel, pronounced *Oo-ree-el*.

Upon opening these curtains you will see through the circular window the night sky brilliant with stars. You may see high before you the pole star, Polaris, with the constellations of the Dragon and the Great and Little Bears revolving round it. Not far away will be a band of light that is the Milky Way. You may be aware also of a darkened landscape before you which is invisible save for the presence of lights of homes and streets and towns that are reflections, in a sense, of the stars above.

Upon the small altar before you will be a golden disc upon which is engraved a series of concentric circles emblematic of the crystalline spheres of the heavens surrounding the Earth. As you pick up this talisman and hold it before you, its circles scintillate with rainbow light of the gems set within it and the very metal of the disc begins to glow in your hands.

And through the window you will see the formation of the Triangle of Earth, downward pointing with a horizontal bar across it. At the bottom point you will see arise the figure of a bull, immensely powerful. Its head alone appears at first but then you may see its whole body in profile, in the form of an ox pulling a mighty plough through the earth. At the upper right the figure of a maiden, who stands among sheaves of corn, and who holds aloft a single ear of corn. And at the upper left the figure of a goat, that appears to plunge out of the sea at the foot of a mountain, and to leap agilely from crag to crag, to stand upon its topmost peak gazing at the stars.

Upon your invoking the name Ghob (pronounced *Gobe*), the ruler of the elemental beings of Earth, you will see the activation of a king and queen of the underworld regions of the earth, in an underground cavern sparkling with gems, and surrounded with gnomes and similar workers within the secret chambers of the earth itself, mining precious metals and stones, and guarding stores of treasure.

When you close down this vision by replacing the golden disc upon the altar, use the spoken formula "In the name of Agla, Uriel and Ghob, I close the gates of the North".

We have now gained some experience of the interior of a magical temple or lodge. We have of course sampled only a small proportion of all possible symbolism that might be met with, but what we have seen and worked with so far gives a general pattern upon which much more can be added as knowledge and experience develops.

All this range of adventure and development is open to the career of the magical students as experience is gained. What we have done is to map out the basic dynamics, in a self-balancing fourfold pattern, that will allow a great deal more symbolism to be built around it.

There are limits however to the use of this kind of mostly inanimate and abstract imagery, and the next stage of the use of the magical imagination is to use it in a more dynamic manner with symbolism that is intelligent, animate and more consciously interactive. This has to do with the formulation and contact of various guides.

We have already sampled something of this in form of the figures that we have met upon the way in our inner journeys, but this has been at a somewhat formal distance, in their form as archetypes of symbolic offices rather than personal contacts in their own right. Our next step therefore is to endeavour to come onto more intimate terms with these focuses of intelligent consciousness upon the inner planes. These may appear in various forms: as totem animals or human guides, or elemental and angelic intelligences of various kinds.

Guardians and Guides

WE HAVE SO FAR learned how to tap the forces of our own aura and to guide our inner energies into forms that, by the process of magical journeys and the formulation of magical shrines, give us a basis for intelligent work upon the inner planes.

So far, however, our work has been mostly with inanimate objects, with the images of landscape and of buildings and of symbols within temple constructs. There is another important factor however in all of this, and that is the presence of animate beings, intelligent sources of guidance and possibly more detailed communication.

It is possible, but unusual, to have an entirely inanimate magical inner scenario. In the work we have done so far we found it helpful to take account of bird song along the trackway as part of our Composition of Mood and of Place. And when we arrived at the tower we met with various animate beings. There was the crowd within the Hall of Welcoming, and more specifically the Smith and the Hermit who took us to the lower levels of the tower, and then the Guide who took us up the spiral stairway and oversaw our efforts with the Temple of the Elements. Each in their way, these figures fulfilled a specific role, as guardian of a particular place and guide to its working.

The simplest form of guide has traditionally been an animal form. This has its parallel in animal totems of various tribal peoples but it has its expression at many levels of being.

One technique that is favoured is to visualise a small animal coming to us as we meditate upon an out-of-doors scenario, perhaps a cave or forest edge. The species of the small animal is a matter of spontaneous choice or individual intuition. For some it may be a domestic creature, such as dog or cat, for others a wild one such as wolf or stag or bear or wise bird. There is no restriction on the type of animal that may appear save the limits of the imagination.

The animal may then lead the way onto an inner journey to a particular shrine or place. When we have been taken to that place the totem animal may then stand as guard outside, waiting to lead us back the way we came, after we have finished our work at the place to which we have been led.

Many examples exist in myth, legend and folklore. An important one that figures in Arthurian legend is that of a king or knight following a stag or a white hart. The animal leads the king or knight far into the forest, away from all his companions until it turns upon its now lone pursuer and exhibits some marvellous property. It may speak, or display some numinous symbol between the branches of its horns. A wild boar is also a common tutelary animal in this kind of story and can lead the hunter into a remote part of an enchanted forest, there to meet some faery being, perhaps a form of the goddess.

One famous example of such is the story of Yvain, or the Knight of the Lion, first recorded by the medieval French romancier Chrétien de Troyes, and which appears also in an ancient Welsh tale included in the collection called *The Mabinogion* as *The Lady of the Fountain*. Here the hero going through the forest is first met and entertained by a young maiden and her widowed father in a castle, where he spends the night, chastely, although not without some hint of romance. The next morning they direct him on his way in search of adventure and he comes upon a giant and grotesque being who is Lord of the Wild Creatures, a sort of guardian over all animal guides. As such he is sometimes likened to the magician Merlin. This being then directs Yvain to the site of the magic fountain.

Here there is an emerald stone set upon four rubies in a stream with a golden cup by its side. He is instructed to pour water from the stream over the stone. As soon as he does so a mighty storm erupts, which, when it has passed, gives way to a paradisal scene with the sun shining and the branches of the trees covered with singing birds. But then a fierce red knight comes galloping up to challenge the newcomer, who if he overcomes this guardian is destined to take his place and become the consort of the faery lady of the fountain.

This story goes back to very ancient rites, and times when sacred places were actually physically guarded in this manner by an armed priest guardian. Sir James Frazer gives an example of one such in *The Golden Bough*. Traditions change according to need and circumstance however, and in Chrétien de Troyes' 12th century version of the story things become more complicated, and another magical creature appears in the form of a lion which helps the knight in his adventures.

You will waste no time in reading widely of myth and legend along these lines for they will stimulate and enrich your magical imagination. This includes all forms of folklore and fairy stories, whether intended for children or adults.

Talking animals play a major role in many children's stories, although there is little direct magical element in the nursery whimsy of some of the tales. However, Mowgli, the jungle boy of Rudyard Kipling, comes close to the mark, and there are many instances, particularly in more traditional tales, where we are very definitely involved with a magical guide, whether it be fish, flesh or fowl.

There is an intermediate category between the animal guide and the human, in the form of one of the 'little folk' as elf or pixie or gnome. A classic example is that of Hob, the overseer of the time travels of the children in Kipling's *Puck of Pook's Hill*. Whether Kipling realised it or not, his story starts with the elements of a magical working. The children are at a specific location associated with the past, a riverside by an old mill (which still stands, for those interested enough to visit his former home of Batemans in East Sussex, which is owned by the National Trust and now open to the public).

The children are performing an evocation of sorts, in that they are dressed up, enacting the fairy parts of *A Midsummer Night's Dream*, and this has the unexpected side effect of evoking to visible appearance the elemental guardian of the place. He teaches them something of their magical and cultural heritage by taking them back through time to previous events in the district, including contacts with the pagan gods such as Weyland the Smith. The means by which this is done is by a short evocation of the three tree powers of oak and ash and thorn.

Kipling found a kindred spirit, and indeed inspiration for much of his involvement in this kind of magical literature, ostensibly for children, in Edith Nesbit, whose *Five Children and It* (originally called *The Psammead*) gives an evocative series of tales with a non-human, non-animal creature, who is able to take them to levels of being off the normal physical plane of experience. Other books of hers involve the children in similar adventures with a phoenix, with an amulet, and with a princess in an enchanted castle. Edith Nesbit had a fairly clear idea of what she was doing from her membership of the Hermetic Order of the Golden Dawn.

Another Golden Dawn related teller of children's tales is P. L. Travers, the author of the Mary Poppins stories, whose original Mary Poppins was more in the nature of a pagan tutelary goddess than as depicted in the later film, as was quickly recognised by magical aficionados of her acquaintance such as the mystical Irish poets W.B. Yeats and George Russell ('A.E.').

A magical type of children's fiction has become an important genre in its own right in the decades since Kipling, Nesbit and Travers wrote, and has developed branches appealing directly to adults, as for instance in the works of Tolkien.

However the 'magical' appeal to the imagination does not stop there, for it can spill over into many kinds of fantasy literature, whether dealing with angelic beings, high elven creatures, ancient civilisations or beings from outer space. It might be said that the twentieth century was a time when a sustained effort was made to expand the mind of the general public with 'mind stretching' forms of entertainment such as this. Started in English fiction in 1895 by H.G. Wells with *The War of the Worlds* and *The Time Machine* and so on, and later adapted to screen and television performance, there is reason to believe that there is some sort of inner purpose in this influx of the marvellous into popular culture.

Not that writers of such material are, by any means, practising magicians, but they are sufficiently imaginative to use their minds in as free and creative a way as any magical student should. Indeed it is arguable that there is as much esoteric truth to be found in contemporary genre fiction as in the learned wisdom teachings of esoteric societies. If this is the case, it is nothing new, for in former times presentations of popular games such as the Tarot contained powerful esoteric information. Magic, therefore, is where you find it, and there is a tradition of presenting esoteric truths in disguised form that goes back at least as far as Apuleius of Madaura's classic comic novel *The Golden Ass,* which at a deeper level is an exposition of the ancient Mysteries of Isis.

Truth can indeed be stranger than fiction, and indeed may sometimes best be presented in the form of fiction. And as often as not, this is through the intuitive insights and subconscious or superconscious promptings that come to popular authors as they delve into their minds for stories. The moral for any esoteric student is to read widely and deeply in imaginative fiction. Much may be ephemeral or inconsequential, but that which is good is likely to stay within your mind as it strikes a resonance with your deeper faculties.

However, to return to the straighter and narrower way of the mainstream of esoteric teachings there is a pantheon of contacts that has come to the fore in much the same period of time as the growth of magical and fantasy fiction. These beings are generally referred to as the Masters, and although their existence was popularised in the late nineteenth century by the publications of the Theosophical Society they are by no means their exclusive invention. Rosicrucian and Masonic documents of the seventeenth century make clear reference to such beings, as do early Jewish Qabalistic writings, where such a contact was called a *maggid.*

In the modern presentation of this type of being a more specific description has been given of some of them, although perhaps their precise form should not be taken in quite so rigid and literal a sense as the stone that Dr Johnson kicked to prove the existence of solid matter. Various schools and writers have since taken up the running and gone on to make their own contacts and publish the results, with varying degrees of worth and credibility.

Taking some of the general descriptions at face value we might come up with a college of inner teachers of wisdom, who measure up something like this:

- The **Master Rakoczi**, sometimes referred to as the Count, and identified or associated with the 18th century Count Cagliostro and the 17th century Francis Bacon. Also credited in other literature with being the Lord of Civilisation, a kind of inner plane function that might be generally equivalent to a kind of inner plane Secretary General of the United Nations.

- The **English Master,** which some have identified with **Sir Thomas More**, Lord Chancellor of England under Henry VIII, who has contrived the distinction of also being a Roman Catholic saint and martyr. The poet Robert Browning is another Englishman reckoned by some to be of Master status. As also **David Carstairs**, an otherwise unknown officer in the British army of the First World War, whose very existence is denied by some biographers, but who has been responsible for some very lively communications.

- The Greek philosopher **Socrates** also appears from time to time, not only in rather abstract philosophical dissertations but in a rather more earthy type of contact in keeping with his personality as revealed in the works of Plato, and his jocular comparison to Silenas, an ancient satyr follower of Bacchus.

- There is a selection of Himalayan based Masters credited with being behind much of the Theosophical teachings of Madame Blavatsky, not least *The Secret Doctrine* and *Isis Unveiled*. Of these the **Master Morya** and the **Master Jupiter**, (whom some link together), have a strong power contact, whilst **Koot Hoomi** is a more gentle influence. Somewhat junior in the Blavatsky pantheon was a Tibetan who has subsequently been credited with a great mass of teaching published by Alice A. Bailey, under the name of **Dwaj Khul**.

- The **Master Serapis**, has Alexandrian Greek connections and has also been used as a channel for elemental and what would nowadays be regarded as 'green' concerns, whilst the **Master Hilarion** has been known to respond to workings of Egyptian magic, as well as in more general communications.

In the modern climate of the importance of feminine power and responsibility it may be asked why all the above mentioned communicators should be male. We suggest that this is not necessarily evidence of sexist chauvinism upon the inner planes, but owes much to the historical context from which we are quoting. Also to be taken into account is that those who made these contacts upon the physical plane were almost always women, so there may well be an element of cross-gender polarity involved in the psychological process of inner plane communication. Not necessarily essential, but possibly helpful.

Be this as it may, in our own approach to these matters we may expect to receive that which we aspire to by our own creative ideas and ideals. The process of communication is like a painted veil, and the pictures upon the veil are painted by us, by means of our own imagination. This does not mean to say that there are no real beings beyond the veil, willing to communicate by means of the pictures we have mutually created in the astral light.

The Masters as we picture them, along with the rest of magical imagery, are all imagination. But that does not mean to say that they are figments of fancy, wish fulfilment or otherwise. If we form an image, and believe in it sufficiently to invest it with some emotive force, then that same image can be overlaid with a similar imaginative projection by an inner plane contact. Once that happens then genuine conscious contact between the planes is possible.

It might be said that this process is automatically followed by many religious devotees, of whatever faith, in their approach to their God or gods or saints, without any conscious concern with magical technique. In this sense, magic is not a cultish minority interest, but a practice that embraces a very wide spectrum of human experience.

The specialist nature of the magical approach is that it attempts a more conscious and detailed form of communication between the planes than is the case with the more generalised approach of the religious devotee.

This does not mean to say that any detailed communication received is going to be foolproof, or even wholly accurate. In mind-to-mind contacts, subjective dubbing in from the subconscious mind of the recipient is a constant factor. This is only to be expected in that the communicator is trying to use the contents of the subconscious mind of the recipient as a kind of word-processor keyboard. When we are attempting such a process we are inviting someone else, the communicator, to think our thoughts for us, or at any rate to direct them. It follows that if we have limited ideas and experience, or our minds are distorted with prejudice or preconceptions, then any communication will be to that extent limited or distorted.

The large proportion of alleged communications that obviously fall short in this respect demonstrate that this is an almost universal problem. One communicator once likened the process to trying to making a picture with feathers, which the slightest draught could disturb, sometimes quite radically. Another has asserted that only 2% of alleged communications are likely to be valid.

However, even if charlatans, dabblers or early learners make up 98% of what has come to be called 'channelled' material, that does not mean to say that 2% do not succeed in getting it right. Our problem lies in identifying that crucial minority. Or in more practical terms, sifting our way through that very broad grey area in between, where communications are like the curate's egg, good or bad in parts. Like long distance radio communication there can be all kinds of interference and fading of signals through inner atmospherics, and inner plane communication has much in common with ham radio.

Some recipients of such communication have worked in full trance, sometimes without any revelation as to who their alleged communicator might be, or with very much conscious sympathy with the process as a whole. One such remarkable case was the clairvoyant Edgar Cayce, who as a conservatively religious man when conscious, did not really have a lot of sympathy with the kind of things he received when he fell into trance, except insofar that they genuinely seemed to help others who came for advice or healing.

It is not our intention to try to teach trance mediumship by means of a book, even if that were possible. As far as higher communications are concerned it is a form of working that is largely superseded. However, the occultist Dion Fortune in a series of early articles in a magazine for her students, did feel it worthwhile to describe the way she went about it. This remains of interest, because the initial stages of the method are very similar to those which we should apply in attempting direct mind to mind telepathic inner contact, without relapsing into the unconscious passive state of mediumistic trance.

As far as she was concerned, the first essentials were complete physical relaxation, relative quietness and subdued light. She found the lowered level of lighting very important, and a condition which seemed to affect the whole aura, for simply blindfolding the eyes was no solution to a problem of too much light. Indeed, any sudden bright light was more disturbing and disruptive even than a sudden loud noise. Once she had got into a trance condition any more or less steady background noise was largely immaterial.

She would then build up in her imagination a picture of the being she wished to contact. This was not just a matter of hard mental concentration, but passing beyond that to what might best be described as a state of almost hypnotic fascination – as in bystanders who have witnessed an accident. All consciousness of the surrounding room would then blank out as she would find herself in full trance.

This could be accompanied by some rather odd sensations. A sense of squinting in the eyes, perhaps due to the eyeballs turning upward as in deep sleep. Then a feeling of going down quickly in a lift. She would blank out for a moment before being aware of herself floating a couple of feet above her physical body, wrapped up like a mummy. Although occasionally, in particularly deep trance, she would find herself standing upright behind the head of her prone physical body, facing the communicator, who was standing by her physical body's feet.

Communication would then commence, and this would tend at first to push consciousness back into her physical body. This was overcome by the will of her own higher consciousness and that of the communicator preventing her lower consciousness from doing so – a process she rather amusingly described as being somewhat like trying to get a reluctant horse into a railway van!

What followed then depended upon the action of the communicator, which was to build up an image of himself and superimpose it upon the medium's body upon the couch, whose vocal chords he would proceed to use to speak to those physically assembled.

Dion Fortune likened this technique to a form of self-hypnosis with the inner communicator taking the part of an unseen hypnotist. When the work in hand was finished she would wake as from a deep sleep remembering very little, and sometimes nothing, of what had occurred. After a certain amount of minor physical discomfort she would find herself considerably invigorated by the experience.

It should be said it took Dion Fortune considerable practice over a number of years to perform all this with ready facility. Apart from this we must remember it also takes two to tango. That is to say, the presence of a communicator willing to come through in this way. It has gone on record that such close association with an entranced physical body is not a wholly pleasant experience, and a matter of duty rather than a pleasure, although most would be too polite to say so. The celebrated remark of one, that the medium's body smelt like an old cough drop, was somewhat by way of an exception.

There has, over the years, been a general rise in consciousness, and acceptance of the reality of inner plane communications, so that some of these heroic efforts by pioneering souls are no longer necessary. A more conscious telepathic or mind-to-mind contact is favoured today, with the recipient fully conscious and seated, rather than prone and unconscious.

Nonetheless a similar modus operandi is involved in the earlier stages, except that the degree of fascinated concentration which brought about projection of consciousness out of the physical body is no longer required. The communicator takes no direct control of physical or etheric organs of the medium, and in token of this the term *medium* has rather given place to *mediator*. The process therefore becomes entirely a matter of conscious visualisation, not dissimilar from the state of mind of a creative writer.

Once a rapport has been built up in conscious cooperation between master and mediator, then there is little mistake about what is happening or any doubts about the reality of the situation. Dion Fortune described the approach of a master as a curious sense of power beginning to develop as if one were waiting for a race to start. With this could come an intuitive awareness as to whom the communicator was likely to be, she being accustomed to work on a regular basis with more than one.

The validity of any communication depends very much on what might be described as the coalescing of the aura of the master with that of the mediator. This is partly a matter of practice, and partly a matter of natural ability, as in any human skill or creative art. The key to success lies in the principle of *like mindedness*.

It is an esoteric axiom, well proven by experience, that upon the inner planes *Like attracts Like.* If therefore we are in sympathy with the aims and expressions of a particular teacher, then we are by that measure more closely attuned to his aura. The practical corollary to this is that if we desire to make an inner contact of any particular kind then we should steep ourselves in whatever appropriate writings we can find that stem from that or a similar source. This is another form of the technique of tuning consciousness.

Esoteric groups perpetuate themselves in this way. Members of the up and coming generation, being instilled with the teaching from the contacts of those who have gone before, are the better placed to make such contacts for themselves. Thus the light of illumination is passed on in that particular school or working group. If, for whatever reason, a hiatus should develop between one generation and another, as long as written material is available, a dedicated individual can use it to renew the contact, and blow the seeming dead ashes into flame.

This can also be helped by knowing the identity of the alleged communicator, so that the visual imagination can be brought to bear in picking up a contact.

In mind-to-mind communication a problem often arises with the speed with which material comes through, generally at twice or three times the rate that would normally be expected if the mediator were working off his or her own resources. Sometimes it may come through more slowly and deliberately in a word for word dictation, but at other times it will come through in small blocks of ideas that have to be instantly rendered into the most appropriate language. At such times the process is very much like taking fast dictation in one language and translating it immediately into another.

Grammar and spelling obviously tend to go by the board in such cases, and even felicity of phrasing and sentence length. This at least needs to be put into order by such light editing as may be necessary. Wherever such communications are destined for wider publication though, particularly in book form, then rather more editing is needed. On the one hand to make the reading easier for those who may not be so committed to teasing out the meaning of complex phraseology; on the other hand to forestall those critics who would readily confuse lack of good English with ignorance or incompetence. However it has to be said that the more editing involved, even by the person who received the material in the first place, the less of the original 'power' of communication comes across.

This matter of 'power' of communication is allied to what Dion Fortune described as the subtle change in the atmosphere that occurs when genuine inner contact is about to take place. It can also happen that the intention behind a particular communication is not primarily in the intellectual content of the message. The intention may be more one of comfort, encouragement or some form of subtle empowerment. In such cases the intellectual content of the communication may be little more than general spiritual commonplace remarks, not necessarily destined for wider publication.

To recapitulate, let us try to draw together some guides for personal action from all these elements that we have considered.

We have established that we can meet beneficent inner guides through the medium of our active imagination. And the power and suitability of these guides can be selected, or filtered out, by means of a traditional symbolic inner environment for them, that we also build in the mind's eye.

If we wish to do so, we may then spend some time in concentrating upon the presence of such a guide, building him – or her – in the creative imagination, getting the general 'feel' of the presence of the inner guide, and waiting to see if any message is expressed.

Messages can come to you in many ways. They may be in the form of words that formulate spontaneously in your mind, or perhaps just a bright idea that springs to life as you contemplate the image of the guide. As an aid to prime the pump, so to speak, it is a very good idea to hold a question in your mind to see if you get an answer. This sets up the most basic form of polarity. And indeed the same principles apply as in outer life, if you wish to start or maintain a conversation then the best way is to ask a question.

It may be thought that all this seems somewhat risky stuff, rather like training yourself into the symptoms of schizophrenia. However the difference between creative visualisation and delusional illness is one of control. The schizophrenic is a victim of hallucinations. We are talking of the controlled use, under will, of our creative powers.

The development of the magical imagination is no different, in essence, from the process cultivated by every imaginative writer and creative artist. Indeed the techniques that we have described could well be used as training for freeing the mind in any form of creative writing.

There is no doubt that some writers are 'guided' or inspired, whether they realise it or not. And it is quite a common occurrence for writers to feel that their characters 'take over' the story. This is not necessarily the same as occult mediation, in which the crucial factor is whether there is a spiritual teacher of merit behind the imaginations involved. But the psychological mechanism is very similar. What matters is who is in the driving seat. And this can be a variety of possibilities from an element in the writer's subconscious to a tuning into some element in the collective unconscious, which might well produce a work of genius irrespective of any esoteric or spiritual content.

Seeking a Guide

The seeking of an inner spiritual guide is very much a personal matter so our directions toward such a step must needs be fairly generalised. We will describe a general outline path or pattern to follow but it is up to you to fill in the detail according to your aspiration and own intuition.

Starting at whatever point you wish in the journey to the tower which we have been using, see yourself being taken by the guide who conducted you to the temple of the elements to a higher storey in the tower. The top of the spiral staircase ends in a door, which he invites you to enter.

When you go through you find yourself in a circular room that is entirely surrounded by windows. The light is clear and comes from all sides, and through the windows you see nothing but the azure of the sky, with perhaps a few wispy clouds. You are above the level of sight of the earth and of the concerns of the tower below you.

The room is bare of furniture except for a small circular table in the centre, of white stone, with two chairs, one on either side that face each other. Sit yourself in one of the chairs. If you look up above you, you will see a circular skylight, in which can be seen not the blue of the sky around you but what appears to be the sun, not exuding heat upon you, but shining with a clear diamond light. In a way that white surface of the table before you is a reflection of the source of light.

You may now find that a book appears before you on the table, in which case you may open it, and regard any pictures that you may see within, or try to read any writing that may appear. Do not strain after this. If it happens, let it happen in its own way and own time, and record and reflect upon what you have seen.

It may be simply that words or ideas or pictures come into your head. If these seem to crystallise of their own accord, and are not psychological baggage of worries or preoccupations that you have brought into this room with you, then these too are worthy of reflection, for they may be another form of communication.

Do not be too much concerned with whom at this stage. The composition of place that you have made will ensure that your contact, even if not consciously recognised, is a valid one. And it can be that it emanates from the light above, which in one sense might be regarded as your personal Holy Guardian Angel.

At some stage you may find that the seat before you becomes occupied. And you can assist it in this way if you wish, by actively building a generalised figure, which you can take from any of the images in the treasurehouse of symbolism known as the Tarot. Be it the Magician, the Fool, the Hermit, the Emperor, the High Priestess, the Empress, or any of the others. They are capable of being utilised by any inner contact who wishes to set up a rapport with you.

Remember that it is you who are in control all the time, no matter how seemingly powerful or eminent a contact may appear to be. You can, at your leisure, simply rise from the table, look up to the bright light of the spirit above, knock upon the table, and leave the room. The guide at the door will see you safely on your way back to normal consciousness.

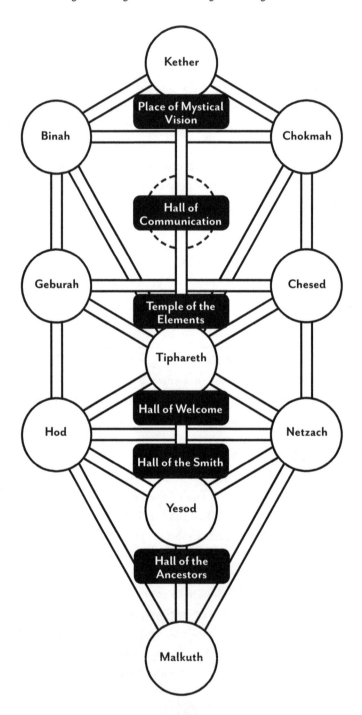

Figure 5: Meditation journey on the Tree of Life

We have now completed our survey of magical images and the magical imagination. You will see that what we have done is to make a journey into your own aura, into the etheric vehicle. Each of the stages on the way in the tower have been a specific part of that aura, not using it directly as in eastern yoga techniques but by making an objective correlative of it, and walking into that space and making contact with any beings we may find or build there.

There is an approximate correlative with both the Tree of Life and the *chakras* of the eastern system, but the correspondences are not exact, for we deal with spheres of influence rather than a rigid set of chinese boxes.

In general terms we entered into the Hall of Welcome more or less as a correlative of the solar plexus centre, with the two lower centres as the hall of the smith and of the ancestors respectively. Then the temple of the elements related to the heart, and the room of communication to the throat, which will open up as experience develops into the head centres.

In terms of the Tree of Life it is probably better to think in terms of triangles of paths rather than specific Sephiroth. Thus the Hall of Welcome is the lower side of Tiphareth and the temple of the elements the higher, which can be thought of as the triangles between Hod-Netzach-Tiphareth and Chesed-Geburah-Tiphareth if you will. The smith's hall is the triangle Netzach-Hod-Yesod and the place of the ancestors the inner side of Netzach-Hod-Malkuth. The hall of communication can be seen as commencing like the triangle between Chokmah, Binah and Tiphareth which is capable of transformation to that between Chokmah, Binah and Kether in the light of experience of the higher modes of inner communication. In Figure 5 we give an outline view of the ground we have covered.

We have now shown you the way through the plethora of magical symbolism in as concise a manner as we think possible. It is now up to you to use your magical imagination in practical steps to tread that way. Thus may imagination transform into reality. And aspiration be elevated into service. God's will be done.

The Threefold Way of the
Lesser Mysteries

THE TREE OF LIFE provides a helpful ground plan of the progress of the Initiate from Earth to Spiritual consciousness. At first, the Way of the Initiate on the Tree of Life is a threefold one, odd though it may seem to be treading three Paths at once. However, Hermes Trismegistus, the patron of magicians and the Hermetic philosophy, was not called 'thrice greatest' for nothing. The situation is plain when we look at the patterns made by the Sephiroth and the Paths that run between them (see Figure 6).

Before we start on our path to the Mysteries, we begin with consciousness rooted in Malkuth, and aim to raise it to awareness of the invisible worlds. This is symbolically depicted on the Tree as treading the 32nd Path toward Yesod and thence by the 25th Path to Tiphareth.

At the same time, like a tightrope walker holding a horizontal pole, we have to keep our functions of expression, represented by Netzach and Hod, in harmonised balance. In the material world, represented by Malkuth in its most mundane aspect, Netzach and Hod represent our emotional and intellectual perceptions respectively; and the corresponding reactions we make to whatever we meet in the course of ordinary social and working life.

As we begin to raise consciousness however, there comes about a change in the way we have to achieve this balance in the dynamic aspects of our consciousness in Netzach and Hod. If we refer to the Tree of Life, this rather complex challenge is laid out with great simplicity.

As we proceed up the 25th Path we need to keep in balance the forces represented by the 29th and 31st Paths until we reach the Sphere of Yesod.

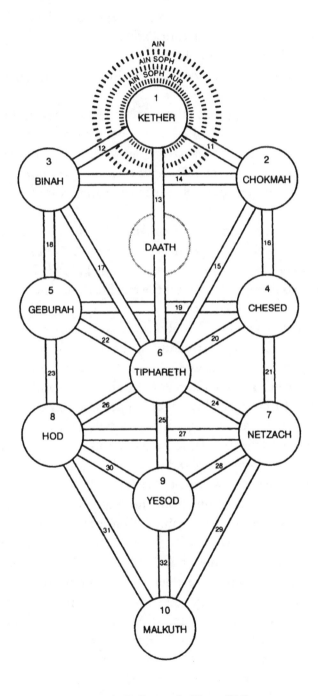

Figure 6: Paths on the Tree of Life

When we reach there we have to begin to balance the forces represented by the 28th and 30th Paths.

There is a kind of crisis point half way up the 25th Path where we cross directly between the two side Sephiroth and this is represented by the 27th Path.

After this, as we approach the higher consciousness in Tiphareth, our balancing act is represented more by the 24th and 26th Paths.

All this may sound very abstract, but there is a great deal of flesh and blood experience that can cleave to these diagrammatic bones. And *realising* and *experiencing* this is what the Path of Initiation is all about.

There are many armchair occultists who may be able to recite the many symbolic correspondences from *The Mystical Qabalah* or *A Practical Guide to Qabalistic Symbolism* like kids used to be able to chant the two times table, but it is the real life experience represented by those symbols that counts.

With such a wealth of symbolism that has become associated with the basically simple structure of the Tree of Life, it is easy to lose touch with the reality. And reality is never more abysmally absent than when students start arguing about the validity of various systems of attribution. When that happens, balance has been lost altogether. The wordy protagonists have fallen off the tightrope to struggle in the labyrinthine intellectual net about the Sephirah Hod. If they start getting heated about it as well then they are floundering in the emotional swamps around Netzach.

To avoid such deviations from the way it helps to keep things very simple. When we have gained a little experience of treading the actual way, then we can begin to indulge in the subtle and sophisticated minutiae about how best to describe it symbolically.

What happens in real life when we start upon the Way? When we feel an urge that becomes so strong that it impels us to search for an esoteric school? This is the stage that is commonly called 'the Seeker,' and the test that is involved is summed up in the Cardinal Virtue of Malkuth, to wit – Discrimination.

When we knock upon the door of a group, or enrol upon its Study Course, we have exercised the virtue of Discrimination in identifying the most appropriate school to answer to our own internal needs. The choice will vary from one Seeker to another. All sheep are not of the same fold.

It is, in one sense, a matter of identifying what we are really seeking. That is the subjective side of Discrimination, based on the adage "Know Thyself." And much depends, according to circumstances, just what training opportunities may be on offer. It may take one or two false shots to find the right one. That is the objective side of Discrimination.

This virtue of Malkuth is the first test on the Path. It is what we have to demonstrate in response to the first intimations from our deeper selves. Of an emotional stimulus from Netzach, an intellectual curiosity from Hod, and the will to do something about it from Yesod.

And so we find ourselves upon a way that seems right for us on a course of formal training. This practical and theoretical instruction is represented by the Paths that lead towards Netzach and Hod. These are the skills we develop on our subjective path in consciousness to Yesod from Malkuth.

Reaching Yesod means we are fully admitted members to a group, initiates actively participating in the work in hand. Collaborating in visualisation work, meditation, ritual, or whatever technical means are employed by the group that we have joined. Holding our own in this environment entails the Cardinal Virtue of Yesod – Independence.

This does not mean that we know it all and can do what we like. There is a long way to go yet and we remain under instruction if we want to arrive at our destination as undamaged goods. However, we are learning to listen to the still small voice of the spirit, our own spiritual will, rather than the calls to conformity with the values of the outer world.

High standards are expected of an initiate of the Right Hand Path. This may be realised if we take a look at the Cardinal Virtues of Netzach and Hod – Unselfishness and Truthfulness.

In the outer world we may be able to get away with a fair amount of self deception (including deception of others). And also self indulgence (often to the detriment of others). But if we elect to aspire to the rules of the Spirit, then as we tread the 25th Path of aspiration higher standards will be expected of us. These higher standards moreover are overseen by a perceptive and demanding Watcher who cannot be fooled. The All-seeing Eye of the Spirit, sometimes depicted as an Eye blazing with glory high up in the Supernal Triangle. So there is no means of dodging the issue, of paying the temple dues with false coin, or laying what is worthless or has been stolen upon the altar of sacrifice.

The immediate goal for which we are making is Devotion to the Great Work within the Sephirah of Harmony and Beauty in Tiphareth. The paths beyond that we need not concern ourselves with now, except to be aware of their existence. They are Intimations of the Higher Worlds, or Intimations of Immortality. Their various Paths and Spheres concern a colloquy with our Holy Guardian Angel who oversees our destiny, with the Inner Plane Adepti behind the lodge, and the various other Spiritual Beings who ascend and descend the Jacob's Ladder that lead to the Supernal worlds of the Spirit.

These higher realms await us. But let us confine ourselves to considerations of our current personality, and how we may best make it a fitting vehicle for service. And let there be no mistake, the only key that opens the way to the higher knowledge is a desire to know in order to serve. Any other motive is self defeating.

This is the form of Discrimination that is exercised by the Guardian of the Threshold who stands at the doorway of the three Paths that lead from Malkuth. The requirement is more than repeating a pious phrase. It is easy enough, after all, to promise not to misuse powers we do not possess. However, once the higher powers are released, and they are very ancient and very strong, wrong use that comes from wrong motivation can put us on the wrong side of a very bleak abyss. In the last analysis therefore, the Dweller on the Threshold is a security guard whose frisking us for right motive is for our own protection.

The ground plan of the Personality can be realised as the kite shaped figure that is formed by the five lower Sephiroth on the Tree of Life. The topmost Sphere within it is the point of contact with the Higher Self, or what is sometimes called the Evolutionary Personality, which in turn is the outer side of our Essential Self and our indwelling Spirit, that Spark from the Divine Fire that is at the heart of our immortality.

With this simple outline in mind we can begin to fill in a selection from the multifarious symbols that can guide us on the way we have to go. As experience grows of the realities that are represented by the symbols, it becomes possible to adopt a more flexible 'pick and mix' approach to them. In the beginning however it is best to stick to just one system, and the one that was evolved by the adepti of the Golden Dawn will suit us very well.

We shall not utilise, however, every jot and tittle of this very complex system. Symbols were made to help us, not to be a burden. So we do not have to drag every item off the shelves of the symbolic supermarket. The pictures of the Tarot Trumps will be enough to begin with, the evocative pictorial images can speak to the Hod and Netzach sides within us.

When we start out in search of experience of the inner worlds, the Tarot image of the World could hardly be more plain in depicting what we are about. We pass into an indigo ovoid, into the unknown as far as the outside world is concerned, but the way is shown by a figure who dances before us, and represents the equilibrium of the contending forces within our own nature and the world outside. On the card this is shown by a hermaphroditic figure holding positive and negative energy fields in each hand, whilst the whole scenario is held in balance by emblems of the Four Holy Living Creatures, from which the Fixed Signs of the Zodiac are derived, indicative of the spiritual principles behind the Four Elements of Earth, Air, Fire and Water.

If we can maintain that kind of balance of the forces within and the forces without, then we will by that very fact traverse the 32nd Path and achieve the Independence of Yesod.

Two other Paths represent the active talents we have to develop as we pass along this way. On the one hand the psychic sensitivity represented by the Moon, and on the other the awakening of intuitive perception that is represented by the Angel announcing the Resurrection.

Psychism is sometimes unjustly denounced by teachers anxious to avoid its worst excesses, which are evident enough in much of pseudo-occult literature. However, it is a faculty that all of us have, and it is a pity to try to cut off some useful organ of our own, just because others may have abused the use of theirs. By virtue of our common humanity we are all aware of atmospheres – be it in the home or the workplace – and psychism is much the same faculty, slightly more developed by our esoteric training.

The nature of these psychic powers is represented by the Moon, the Ruler of Flux and Reflux. Dion Fortune evokes this kind of consciousness very well in some of her descriptions in *The Sea Priestess*. It is a form of perception in a state between waking and sleeping, again as Dion Fortune has remarked on many occasions, and its twilight ambience is clearly represented by the canine animals on the card, of dog and wolf, for in idiomatic French the phrase *entre chien et loup* – between dog and wolf – is used to describe the twilight.

The other talent is that of the ability to be astonished or enlightened. To crack open the structures of the concrete mind, the sepulchres of preconceived ideas, to let in a little inspiration. To bring release to the spirits in prison, all those truths that have been ignored, rejected or suppressed. Our response to the blast of the angelic trumpet is a first step on the road to the Virtue of Truthfulness in Hod, not that this may not prove to be a somewhat scorching experience, as the disciples found on the day of the first Pentecost, and Saul on the road to Damascus.

Once we have become established in what is sometimes called the Temple of Yesod, we have achieved the realisation of the reality of the inner planes. We are not entirely reliant on other people telling us what they are about, even if our sight may still be a little dim in these early stages.

Three more Paths now confront us. How are we going to raise consciousness further? We have learnt the rudiments of the skills of the initiate, how do we develop and use them?

Before us lies the 25th Path of aspiration that leads to the goal of Tiphareth, whose virtue is Devotion to the Great Work. If your first devotion is to anything else then you had better be content to remain where you are. There is honourable service to be given in the Lesser Mysteries but the Great Work entails being commissioned to the responsibilities of adepthood. That is, to office in the Greater Mysteries, and the perceptions of evolutionary consciousness rather than those of the personality currently in incarnation.

The road to this condition is the 25th Path, sometimes called the Path of the Arrow, that is represented by a rainbow, the divine bow of promise, and a winged angel pouring an elixir from one vessel to another. It is another version, a transformation, of the dancing figure in the emblem of the World, now lifted to a higher arc. Still holding a balance between two forces, but now mixing them in just proportion, as the name Temperance signifies.

The two side Paths here are also more aspirational than their equivalents that led out of Malkuth. They are represented by the Sun and the Star. The Sun that beams down from Hod is the bright light of self evident spiritual truth, a light by which all dark places are enlightened. The Star is the realisation and feeling of divine beauty that comes from Netzach. It is closely associated with Venus, where the pattern of the Earthly Paradise is said to be held. These aspirations for Truth and Beauty therefore flank the path of Aspiration that leads to higher consciousness.

But aspiration on its own is not enough. Aspiration alone can be but wish fulfilment fantasy unless we have the will and ability to bring it to realisation and fulfilment. This is implied by the transverse path across our way; its symbol – the Lightning-struck Tower. Aspiration alone might be regarded as our being enclosed in an ivory tower, and many are the occult-tasters rather than occultists who remain in this condition. High on great thoughts but low on practical achievement.

If we are to progress to be responsible servers of the higher powers in the Temple of Tiphareth, the sphere of God Made Manifest in the Sphere of Mind, then we have to be prepared for the lightning flash of illumination, or the lightning strike of destruction of false values.

This may come to us as a shock, but it is also a form of enlightenment and of tapping heavenly energy. It can, however, be a controlled and directed part of the initiation process. Observe that the top of the tower is gently lifted up to receive the bolt from the empyrean. The old ludibrium of *The Chymical Marriage of Christian*

Rosencreutz elaborates upon this, for within the alchemical tower it is a means of restoring new life to the sacrificed king and queen.

It is here that what we said earlier about right motive comes more to the fore. Seeking heavenly powers and knowledge for personal ends will result, not in new life, but in being cast down in a shower of falling masonry.

And so we may now approach the upper reaches of the 25th Path, which is where the Lesser Mysteries begin to pass into the Greater. For whoever can enter the Temple of Tiphareth as of right as an adept (albeit a minor one) rather than being invited as an oblate under instruction, or as a temporary guest, will of necessity pass into the consciousness of the Higher Self.

This is to enter into a wider air, and also to experience a change of attitude. For we shall be measuring our current life in terms of evolution rather than our current incarnation. By this we mean a real change of consciousness – not a mere intellectual appreciation or emotional impression of what it might be like. We are speaking of the consciousness of the Adept, which is represented by the six rayed star, the fusion of the triangles of higher and lower consciousness.

This entails experience of the highest pair of balancing paths, one of which is represented by Death and the other by the Devil.

These images may seem menacing, even portentously so. Yet the reality is more prosaic, although no less difficult to face. The Cardinal Virtue of Netzach is Unselfishness – taken to a condition of unreserved dedication that implies a death to the interests of the Lower Self. Similarly the Cardinal Virtue of Hod is Truthfulness – and that means looking at things as they really are – and that can seem the very Devil.

One is reminded of the admonitions of two of the Masters to some members of the Fraternity of the Inner Light in its very early days, some ninety years ago, when the standard of applicant was not very high, but through the unique powers of mediumship of Dion Fortune they could converse with the Masters direct.

To one who had her own ideas of what she wanted to contribute to the work, after a searching conversation which demonstrated that her assumptions were delusory, she was told: *"It is more important to do what is wanted than what you want to do."* That is the meaning of the Unselfishness of Netzach.

The other, addressed to some unrealistic idealists who thought the Master's teaching insufficiently elevated, was

> "You cannot evade facts, my children. We may just as well face them. You
> may say 'these things are deplorable, is there anything that can be done?' But
> you cannot say they are not so, and that is why we train you; because the
> tendency of the spiritually minded is to be nice minded. Now we do not want
> you to be nice minded, we want you to be true minded. There is a distinction."

That is one meaning of the demonic image that exemplifies the Path from the Truthfulness of Hod.

Beyond the consciousness of Tiphareth there proceeds a seven-fold Path represented by the five Paths that proceed upwards from that Sephirah upon the Tree and the two that trace the line of the Pillars of Manifestation to right and left, bringing the intimations of the Holy Guardian Angels and the Masters directly into the Incarnationary Personality.

The Sevenfold Way of the Greater Mysteries

T HE WAYS TO higher consciousness are shown upon the Tree of Life by the paths that proceed upward from Tiphareth, the central Sephirah whose virtue is Devotion to the Great Work.

That Great Work, to quote an old ritual, is an operation "that God undertakes in the soul of man – to wit, Regeneration."

Regeneration also signifies rebirth. Thus the achievement of higher consciousness whilst still within the Earthly personality is often called a Second Birth, and those who have experienced it the Twice-born.

The way to this experience is not necessarily a blinding and debilitating flash of revelation as experienced by St Paul on the road to Damascus. It probably came in that fashion to this great soul because the assumptions and preconceptions of his worldly personality, conditioned by heredity and environment as a pious Pharisee, were causing him to persecute rather than to embrace what was to be his life's work. He had a high spiritual destiny to perform of spreading the Light of Christ from the confines of what was then still a small Jewish sect to the Gentile world at large.

We all have a spiritual destiny to discover and perform even if it be not as far reaching or spectacular as that of St Paul. The knowledge of our own particular segment of the Divine Plan is held within the recesses of our own Essential Self. It is this knowledge that we are enjoined to seek in the ancient Mystery injunction to "Know Thy Self!"

For most of us the process is a gradual and a painstaking one, a pilgrimage that extends over a sequence of lifetimes. In a series of personalities projected into the world we seek to discover and express the ideals of our own particular destiny – in the unfolding of the evolution of consciousness in the Solar Logoidal Plan. The higher Paths and Spheres upon the Tree of Life help us to appreciate, within our lower consciousness, the pattern of these higher powers within our own Essential Self.

The Essential Self is a twofold being, and is thus represented by two higher triangles upon the Tree.

The upper triangle (Kether – Chokmah – Binah) signifies our immortal Spirit whose roots lie in the Cosmos or the Divine Mind, the Limitless Light.

The lower triangle (Chesed – Geburah – Tiphareth) signifies that part of consciousness that lasts for an evolution and is called by a variety of names by different schools: the Higher Self, the Soul, the Evolutionary Personality.

Upon the Tree of Life the point of contact between higher and lower consciousness lies in the sphere of Tiphareth, which is sometimes called the Egoic Lotus in other traditions. The purpose of the Mysteries is that, by meditation and ceremonial observance, we may gradually open up the petals of that lotus. By these means we begin to express within the lower world something of the power, love and wisdom of our higher powers that are rays from the spiritual light.

In terms of Qabalistic symbolism, the opening of those petals is imagined as the opening of a number of gates, each of which lead on to a particular Path in higher consciousness leading on to the upper reaches of the Tree of Life. These Paths are seven in number and the treading of them may thus be called the Sevenfold Way of the Greater Mysteries.

Five of them proceed from Tiphareth (the aspirational side of our worldly personality) and a further two ascend from Hod and Netzach (our lower mind and emotions respectively). The flow is, however, a two-way one, for consciousness manifests at every level by an interchange of polarities. So we may look upon the Paths not only as ways of upward-looking aspiration but at the same time as channels of down-flowing inspiration.

As before, when we contemplated the lower Paths in 'the Threefold Way of the Lesser Mysteries', we do best to keep things simple to begin with, fixing upon a few basic ideas and images from the vast treasure house of traditional symbolism.

Tiphareth, the sphere of harmony and beauty, has a dual function, for it represents the highest point of our aspiring Incarnationary Personality as well as the lowest point of our Evolutionary Personality. The three principle magical images of Tiphareth give some idea of the process of dawning higher consciousness: in the Child, the King and the Sacrificed God. This crucial sphere is a veritable temple of interchange, a rainbow bridgehead between the upper and lower worlds. It is not for nothing that it is aligned, in terms of the etheric vehicle, with the human heart; and the spiritual worth of a person might very well be measured by the capacity of 'heart' that they demonstrate in their relationship to other creatures in the outer world.

There are, however, two flanking Paths. They are aligned with the Dark and Bright Pillars of Function, and do not pass through the centralising focus of consciousness at Tiphareth. They are the 21st Path between Chesed and Netzach and the 23rd Path between Geburah and Hod. These two paths are the channels for direct realisations from higher consciousness dropped into the intellectual mind of Hod or into the seat of ideals of Netzach within the human personality.

The human personality is never left without guidance and these are ways by which the Essential Self endeavours to guide the personality within the world by enlightenment and charity. This process occurs within every human being, whether or not they are consciously attempting to open themselves to higher consciousness via Tiphareth through esoteric or religious belief and practice. Realisations received in this way may seem self evident to them or determine their particular goals and assumptions in life.

In the nature of things there is a certain difference of perception between ideas and ideals that have their origin in the higher worlds and those which owe their origin to experience and expediency within the lower worlds. This is shown by the reversed attitude of the Hanged Man between Geburah and Hod. Similarly the turn of the Wheel of Fortune between Chesed and Netzach indicates that desires pertaining to the higher worlds are not necessarily congruent with the natural desires and appetites of the incarnate personality.

We come to a more conscious awareness of these intimations of the higher worlds if we centre our consciousness in Tiphareth, which is the sphere of conscious dedication and aspiration, as expressed by its cardinal virtue, Devotion to the Great Work.

As far as the Sephiroth immediately above it are concerned it can be helpful if we objectify them as force fields of the consciousness of particular types of inner plane being. Thus we may consider Geburah to be the sphere of the Holy Guardian Angels and Chesed as the sphere of those human guiding intelligences who are commonly known as the Masters.

Within these spheres of consciousness we each have our own unique Holy Guardian Angel (who holds the particular part of the Divine Plan that is our own spiritual destiny) and a Master to whom we owe particular allegiance through spiritual type or dedicated service.

Thus we may see the 22nd Path between Tiphareth and Geburah as a channel for conscious co-operation with our own Holy Guardian Angel, as compared to the unconscious intimations that may come via the 23rd Path.

Similarly the 20th Path between Tiphareth and Chesed can be a channel for more conscious co-operation with our own particular Master (or Masters) as compared to the influence from this source channelled to us unconsciously via the 21st Path.

Influences that come down to us through the side Paths are likely to be mediated to us upon a group level as a kind of general moral ambience whereas those which come through Tiphareth are likely to be more conscious and individualised to our particular abilities and needs. Our reaction to the higher intimations that come directly into mind or emotions via the side Paths will depend upon how far in our personality we naturally reflect the cardinal virtue of each of the basal Sephiroth – respect for Truth in the intellectual world of Hod and expression of Unselfishness in the emotional world of Netzach.

In the more consciously aspirational approach to higher consciousness via Tiphareth we find five gates confronting us. The 13th Path to and from Kether, the 15th Path to and from Chokmah, the 17th Path to and from Binah, the 20th Path to and from Chesed and the 22nd Path to and from Geburah.

In practical terms we might visualise ourselves as being within a golden temple adorned with the traditional symbolism of Tiphareth. Then, as a means of focusing our spiritual aspirations, we may look towards one or other of the gates to the Paths, each one of which has a traditional guide who is also a guardian who may be represented by one of the icons of the Tarot Trumps.

The one who stands at the gate of the 22nd Path to Geburah may thus be visualised in the traditional figure of Justice – a maiden with a sword and pair of scales. In some schools this has led to this Path being associated with karmic adjustment, and to it even being called "the terrible 22nd Path". So St Paul may have found it on the way to Damascus, but only because he was badly oriented in his personality to begin with. The figure of Justice does not necessarily represent any terrible retribution for past misdeeds but can lead us to the knowledge and conversation of our Holy Guardian Angel who holds the perfect pattern of our particular part within the Divine Plan. By her sword she indicates our true path in life, as straight as the blade and as narrow as its edge; whilst her balance signifies the need to deviate neither to the left nor to the right in our spiritual quest. The symbols also have a very positive aspect. The sword represents our own faith and spiritual will, and the scales the faculties of discretion and discrimination whereby we can measure within our lives a true and balanced approach to whatever may confront us.

When we turn our eyes toward Chesed we turn our aspirations towards another great force-field of higher influence, to the great guiding souls of humanity, amongst whom will be numbered our own particular Master, (as also the saints of the Church for the devout). This guide to this sphere of realisation is well represented by the image of the Hermit, standing upon a mountain top with staff of faith and power and guiding lantern.

We do not have to become involved in a labyrinth of intellectual speculation about the validity of ancillary Qabalistic symbolism. Realisations regarding that may well come with experience but in the first instance, we can make a very worthwhile and rewarding step by simply opening our hearts and minds to the Holy Guardian Angel and the beloved Master through the imagery of Justice and the Hermit respectively.

Having established some kind of realisation of what these higher spheres signify, we might spare a thought for the great 19th Path that interconnects them, a Path of Love in action, where Power and Wisdom effectively expressed in interaction through the image of the Maiden holding in check the Lion. The title of the relevant Tarot card is Strength – signifying spiritual strength, power and control – and which also gives a hint as to the importance of the Divine Feminine within the scheme of things.

In this central triangle upon the Tree of Life of Tiphareth – Geburah – Chesed and the Paths that interconnect them we have an emblem of our own Higher Self or Evolutionary Personality, that can be expressed in terms of the image making faculty of our Incarnationary Personality.

It would be a mistake, however, on the grounds that it is too remote for conscious consideration, for us to ignore the Spirit that rests within each one of us. It is, after all, the root and foundation of our very being. In terms of the Tree of Life it is represented by the supernal triangle (Kether – Chokmah – Binah) and from our aspirational base in Tiphareth there are three ways to it, via the 14th 15th and 17th Paths.

Following the simple system that we have devised for our work so far we might regard Binah as the sphere which contains the pattern of the Seven Spiritual Ray types. We might even formalise it as a Temple of the Seven Rays.

Admittedly, the very of use pictorial symbolism means that we are working at a level below the spiritual. However, the magic mirror of the visual imagination when rendered still and clear by mind training is a means whereby the spiritual can be validly *reflected*. In a similar way spiritual truths may be rendered meaningful to the personality by means of parables and symbolic allegories. We can buttress this with intellectual speculation as much as we wish, for instance by study of books of esoteric cosmology and metaphysics, such as *The Cosmic Doctrine*, Blavatsky's *Secret Doctrine*, or Alice Bailey's five volume *Treatise on the Seven Rays*. However, such cerebral instruction, although ever worthwhile, is designed to train the mind as much as to inform it.

In simpler terms we can realise a great deal by just visualising the Seven Rays in terms of colours of the rainbow, each mediated by a mighty shadowy presence who embodies the spiritual principle behind each one. Such might be called Ray Exemplars, or even species of Archangel in traditional theology. They also have a distinct resemblance to the Valar in Tolkien's *Silmarillion*.

To make some kind of approach to what has sometimes been called the *concrete spiritual* level of our own innermost being then we might well invoke the presence of the goddess or priestess of Love, who stands at the portal of the 17th Path that conjoins Tiphareth and Binah. We may see the two Lovers as representative of our own Higher and Lower Self which seek to be led by the winged Cupid towards that concourse of spiritual forces in the heavens. There, a particular colour or combination of colours, perhaps in the form of a crystal, with resonances of a particular traditional planetary type, or note upon the harmonic scale, may provide a representation of the spiritual type of our own Divine Spark. A traditional Qabalistic name for this experience is the Sanctifying Intelligence with the cardinal virtue of Silence, beyond the clamour of the form worlds.

We are well beyond the lower worlds of form at this level, as is shown by the direct connection between Evolutionary Personality and Spirit upon the 18th Path, with its symbol of the Charioteer. This is the stuff of the Vision of Ezekiel and whereby great souls such as Elijah ascended to heaven. In a more femininely oriented metaphysic it can also be represented by Winged Victory in her triumphal car. Dante's vision of the triumphal procession in the Earthly Paradise at the conclusion of *The Purgatorio* is also an evocative description of this.

If we turn now to the opposite pole of our spirit, represented by the sphere of Chokmah, we find ourselves in the Sphere of the Fixed Stars. A star is no bad image for the Divine Spark within each one of us, that is formed by the dance of the Cosmic Atom within the Mind of God in the Limitless Light beyond the Veils of the Unmanifest. Some inkling of this kind of consciousness may be dimly gleaned when we contemplate the grandeur of the night sky.

In so doing we can evoke the twelve-fold symbolism of the zodiac if we will, although the starry wisdom is more comprehensive than that, for the number of traditional holy constellations is forty-eight, and the Milky Way and Circumpolar Stars, as those of the great Celestial Sea of the Southern Hemisphere, also have their spiritual significance and teaching. This spiritual experience of Chokmah, this sphere of the stars, is traditionally called the Illuminating Intelligence, and it inspires and indeed compels the virtue of Devotion. Here it is not just Devotion to the Great Work, which is but the means to an end. Devotion here is to the beginning and end itself, the Alpha and Omega, the Spiritual Fountainhead beyond the Crown of Creation – the Ain Soph Aur or Limitless Light.

The Path between Chokmah and Tiphareth upon the Tree of Life, the 15th, has as its guide and custodian a mighty king, called in Tarot terms the Emperor. He may be regarded as the archetypal Lord of Wisdom and Builder of the Temple exemplified by King Solomon. The Hebrew Letter allocated to this Path, ה *Heh*, meaning a Window, signifies a window into spiritual consciousness.

The direct connection between Spirit and Evolutionary Personality, the 16th Path that conjoins Chesed and Chokmah, has an allied figure, the High Priest or the Grand Master of the Mysteries, connecting the sphere of the Masters of Wisdom with the Wisdom of the Stars.

At the summit of the Tree of Life is the Crown of Creation. This is the closest we can conceive of that part of us which is closest to the Divine Mind. It is called the Admirable or Hidden Intelligence and its traditional virtue the Attainment of the Great Work. From it depend two Paths, the 11th and the 12th, one represented by a Fool and the other by a Magician. These are two aspects of the Spirit in polar manifestation. In the one case the pure innocence of the spirit entering the manifest star ways. In the other the spirit expressing itself through a combination of the Seven Rays.

Conjoining these two complementary modes of manifestation is the 14th Path, whose Tarot Image is the fruitful feminine image of the Empress. She sits in the midst of fruitfulness, and the additional symbolism of her Path are Venus and the Hebrew letter *Daleth* ד, signifying a Door. In traditional teaching Venus holds the true pattern for all life on Earth as it seeks achievement as a spiritual planet. The doorway may thus be regarded as the Golden Gates which lead to the Garden of Eden restored, the Earthly Paradise.

A direct way to this mystical realisation is represented by the 13th Path joining Tiphareth (the heart of the Evolutionary Personality and aspirational point of the Incarnationary Personality) with Kether (the fount of the Spirit in manifestation). The guardian/guide of this Path is represented by the High Priestess, seated before a veil between two pillars, with a scroll of wisdom in her hands, and the receptive and reflective Moon at her feet. A hint of the fruitfulness that lies above is contained upon the pattern of figs and pomegranates upon the veil behind her. She is the universal goddess Isis, in Christian terms represented by the Blessed Virgin, the bringer to birth of spiritual powers in Earth, the supreme mediatrix between heaven and earth.

Filled with the Devotion to the Great Work in Tiphareth, we may cross the desert, negotiate the wilderness, sail over the abyss that divides spiritual force from material form, until we reach the spiritual oasis of the transverse 14th Path. Here we may find her transformed into the bountiful Eve restored, within a fruitful and blossoming Garden of Eden, at the centre of which is the pure spiritual intelligence of Kether, the rock from which flows the fount of the four rivers of manifest creation.

The process of raising consciousness directly to spiritual levels upon the 13th Path is a mystical journey that is also known as the Uniting Intelligence. But by whichever route we travel, once this union is achieved, we complete a spiritual circuit whereby Spirit and Higher and Lower Selves are conjoined. In this blaze of illumination we may pass back into the greater Limitless Light of the Cosmos, returning home with the treasures of experience within the Solar Logoidal system, to the enrichment of the Divine Mind of which ultimately we all form a part.

Qabalistic Pathworking in the Western Esoteric Tradition

THE Western Esoteric Tradition is a useful term in which to describe a broad range of efforts towards spirituality outside of the established parameters of organised religion. By comparison the Eastern Esoteric Tradition – although also applied to the western world – represents similar efforts that derive their inspiration from eastern religious or philosophical sources, whether Buddhism, Hinduism or various forms of yoga, including such westernised interpretations as Theosophy.

The Western Esoteric Tradition, on the contrary, looks toward specifically western speculative movements. These can be within the Christian tradition, or the largely 18th century Deism that informs a great deal of Freemasonic symbolism, or the Rosicrucian and alchemical traditions of an earlier period. Above all however, throughout all periods, there is the element of Jewish mysticism that is known (under various conventions of spelling) as Qabalah. The word, broadly translated, means "received wisdom".

Whilst playing a long term peripheral role in Hebraic religion, for various cultural and historical reasons the Qabalah has not been readily accessible to the gentile world, not least because of its great diversity and a lack of competent translations. In Renaissance times the philosopher prince Pico della Mirandola brought some attention to it as a means by which the Jews might be converted to Christianity – a point of view that did not win him much favour either from the orthodox Christian or Jewish worlds.

The Qabalah later resurfaced in the 17th century particularly in diagrammatic form, with apologists of the Rosicrucian movement, and the evocative diagrams of Robert Fludd, and various exponents of psycho-spiritual interpretations of alchemy have remained a popular source of illustration for esoteric books to this day.

There things rested until the middle of the 19th century when the French occultist Alphonse Louis Constant, writing under the Hebraicised pen name of Eliphas Levi, published his *Dogme de la Haute Magie* and *Rituel de la Haute Magie* later translated by A.E. Waite under the portmanteau title of *Transcendental Magic*. Each book was divided into twenty-two chapters, each chapter being accorded one of the twenty-two letters of the Hebrew alphabet.

This was also the first published allocation of the twenty-two letters of the Hebrew alphabet to the twenty-two Trumps of the Tarot. This popular game of cards of Italian Renaissance origin had gained a certain reputation over the previous fifty years as a fortune telling device, a certain historical and metaphysical glamour having been accorded them in *Le Monde Primitif*, a French encyclopaedic work of 1773-82 which speculated that they derived from a book of ancient Egyptian magic.

Eliphas Levi's imagination, stimulated by this, led him to seek various symbolic attributions between Tarot and Qabalah. This in turn formed the basis for further elaboration of French esoteric theory in the latter years of the nineteenth century, particularly at the hands of Dr Gerard Encausse, in *Le Tarot des Bohemians* of 1889, written under the pen name of Papus. The title implies the cards have a special connection with the gypsies but this assumption has been disputed. A scholarly investigation of the origins of the occult Tarot has since been published in *A Wicked Pack of Cards* by Decker, Depaulis and Dummett (St. Martin's Press, New York, 1996).

In the English speaking world the Qabalistic side of the Western Esoteric Tradition came largely under the influence of the esoteric society founded in 1888 that is generally referred to as the Hermetic Order of the Golden Dawn although it developed various branches with various names. In some respects a descendent of masonic and esoteric antiquarian bodies such as the Societas Rosicruciana in Anglia it developed a practical side and mode of teaching that was largely inspired by researches in the British Museum by one of its founding members, S.L. MacGregor Mathers.

Mathers had also been influenced by the teaching of the

charismatic animal rights campaigner and visionary Anna Kingsford who, in 1881, with her colleague Edward Maitland, gave a series of lectures that made an enormous impression upon contemporary esoteric London society and was published as *The Perfect Way*. She included references to the Qabalah in her teaching and Mathers dedicated his book *The Kabballah Unveiled* to her. This work of his was a translation from the Latin *Kabballah Denudata* of Knorr von Rosenroth, which was itself a translation of parts of the late medieval Qabalistic text *Zohar*, or *Book of Splendour.*

Baron Spedalieri, an influential follower of Eliphas Levi, was enthused enough to proclaim that Anna Kingsford's work completely surpassed all previous Qabalistic teaching. There are many Hebraic scholars who might validly dispute this contention, but what the Baron no doubt had in mind was that she was the first to provide some kind of introductory guide that was accessible to a modern gentile audience. One of Mathers' associates, Dr. Wynn Westcott, produced a translation of another Qabalistic text, the *Sepher Yetzirah*, or *Book of Formations* but no practical explanatory work upon the subject was to appear in accessible form until 1932 with Israel Regardie's *A Garden of Pomegranates* and Dion Fortune's *The Mystical Qabalah* of 1935.

We must also take account of an important interim figure, Aleister Crowley, a colourful character with a number of well publicised personal shortcomings, who, albeit in highly priced limited private editions, published various elements of Golden Dawn teaching in his serial work *The Equinox* in the first decade of the 20th century. He was also responsible for an important little work of 1909, *Seven Seven Seven*, that was a book of tables of symbolic correspondences between various symbol systems, using the Tree of Life of the Qabalah, which is a handy diagram upon which to classify and compare symbols and terms from a variety of different mythological, religious and philosophical systems.

The system of ten spheres represents ten aspects of the emanation of God from the All Highest, the Fount of all Creation at the top, to the holy presence of God on earth as the Shekinah. As such it is a very holy device for the worship and understanding of their God by Hebrew mystics. Gentile exegesis as found in the Western

Esoteric Tradition is more prosaic, looking upon it more as a virtual philosophical and psychological card index system.

Between the ten spheres, or Sephiroth, are the twenty-two interconnecting paths representing the relationship between any two of the spheres, and to these, in the ancient Qabalistic texts such as the *Sepher Yetzirah,* are allocated the twenty-two letters of the Hebrew alphabet – which in Hebrew orthography also serve as numbers.

It is these twenty-two paths which in the course of the remainder of the twentieth century became analysed and exploited as aids to mystical and occult experience and psychological analysis with a metaphysical and spiritual dimension, as we have seen in Chapter 7.

Plainly the field that opens before us is a vast one, that aims to comprehend the soul of man and of the universe and everything that therein is: physical, metaphysical, psychological and mystical. For now, let us take the bottom one of all, which leads between the 10th and the 9th spheres. In modern esoteric thought these are commonly held to represent consciousness of the material world (the 10th sphere, Malkuth, the Kingdom) and consciousness of what is usually referred to as the subconscious mind (the 9th sphere, Yesod, the Foundation).

If we turn to any of the texts that are now available we will find a general agreement as to the principal symbols. The Hebrew letter is the 22nd one, ת *Tau,* which means a cross or mark; for each letter has a particular name, as well as a number. The number of Tau is 300. The Tarot Trump that is allocated to the Path is the 22nd Trump, known as the World. An astrological sign is also part of the principal system and for this path it happens to be the planet Saturn.

The general method of going about a journey along the Path is to start with the Tarot Trump, regarding it as a picture through which one has to pass, and then midway down the Path to come upon the configuration of the Hebrew letter, and finally at the end of the Path to meet the astrological figure. Thus in the case of the 32nd Path between Malkuth and Yesod we have first the World, then Tau, and finally Saturn. However, we must not forget the beginning and ending spheres that form the poles of this experiential journey. Malkuth is identified with the Earth, as one might expect for a sphere that is attributed to physical sensory consciousness; Yesod is identified with the Moon, poetically described as the mistress of tides not only within the objective but within the subjective sphere.

Dion Fortune has described it well in one of her novels, *The Sea Priestess,* as the protagonist of her story sinks towards subconscious mentation while lying, partly drugged by medication for asthma, looking at the moonrise through his bedroom window:

> Now I cannot tell what I said to the Moon, or what the Moon said to me, but all the same, I got to know her very well. And this was the impression I got of her – that she ruled over a kingdom that was neither material nor spiritual, but a strange moon-kingdom all of her own. In it moved tides – ebbing, flowing, slack water, high water, never ceasing, always on the move; up and down, backwards and forwards, rising and receding; coming past on the flood, flowing back on the ebb; and these tides affected our lives. They affected birth and death and all the processes of the body. They affected the mating of animals, and the growth of vegetation, and the insidious workings of disease. They also affected the reactions of drugs, and there was a lore of herbs belonging to them. All these things I got by communing with the Moon, and I felt certain that if I could only learn the rhythm and periodicity of her tides I should know a very great deal. [1]

The treading in visualisation of the 32nd Path should therefore be another way of approaching, in controlled healthy consciousness (not induced by drugs or illness), the inner world behind sensory consciousness. We should also be prepared to accept that this is not merely a subjective world, but that it has an objective side to it.

In trying to describe the nature of the 32nd Path I do not think I can improve upon that which I wrote some fifty years ago:

> This Path joins Malkuth, the physical world, and Yesod, the universal unconscious and etheric web which forms the foundation of physical existence. It is therefore a Path of introversion from the sensory consciousness to the consciousness of the deeps of the inner world. When one treads it one is boring down into the unconscious mind and many and strange are the things that one may meet there.

---

1 Dion Fortune, *The Sea Priestess,* [Weiser, Boston, 2003] p.5

It is like the hole in the earth into which Alice fell, leading to her strange adventures in Wonderland. It is also, on a mythological level, the way down to the Underworld, trod by Oedipus at Colonos, Orpheus in search of Eurydice and many others, but primarily it is Persephone's descent into the world of Pluto, the King of the Underworld. Alice, indeed, might be said to be a modern version of Persephone, for Carroll was a writer who wrote of the deeps of the unconscious mind.

The Path is also the way of psycho-analysis and shows the difference between the Freudian and Jungian techniques, for when the unconscious images of Yesod are met with, the Freudian tries to analyse them with reference to life history in Malkuth, daily living, but the Jungian process follows the images through until they become symbols of transformation leading to the psychic harmony of Tiphareth. In other words, the Jungian technique is, or should be, a pressing on to the 25th Path, Yesod–Tiphareth, after the way-in, the 32nd Path, Malkuth–Yesod, has been trodden.[2]

Indeed that further progression beyond the subconscious sphere of Yesod could be equated with the eventual revelation of the Jungian archetype of the Self, in Tiphareth. However, let us take but one step – or one Path – at a time, in order to make the method of progress clear. Public exegesis now being rather more available than it was in former days, we can make a comparison to see how three different practitioners of the Western Esoteric Tradition go about the treading of the 32nd Path.

We will cite, in order of publication, first my own in *Experience of the Inner Worlds*,[3] then Charles Fielding in *The Practical Qabalah*,[4] and finally Dolores Ashcroft-Nowicki in *The Shining Paths*.[5] All three follow the system of attributions favoured by Dion Fortune and Israel Regardie in the wake of the Golden Dawn tradition; however, it will be seen that upon the formal structure of symbolism a certain amount of spontaneous imaginative vision occurs, which

---

2 Gareth Knight, *A Practical Guide to Qabalistic Symbolism* [Red Wheel/Weiser, Boston, 2001] Vol.2 *On the Paths and the Tarot* p. 1-2
3 Gareth Knight, *Experience of the Inner Worlds*, [Skylight Press, Cheltenham, 2010] pp. 206-210
4 Charles Fielding, *The Practical Qabalah*, [Weiser, York Beach, 1989] pp. 61-65
5 Dolores Ashcroft-Nowicki, *The Shining Paths*, [Aquarian Press, Wellingborough, 1983] pp. 19-27

will differ for each practitioner, but nonetheless be within the general metaphysical and psychological ambience of the Path concerned.

The convention is to start within a visualised location that is usually in the form of a simple temple, thus providing a spiritualised ambience to what is to take place, placing it somewhat above the personal psychological concerns of everyday life. Thus in my own working I chose to visualise a circular space surrounded by a grove of black pillars shot with gold, with a black and white chequered paving between. Within the centre was an altar in the form of a double cube, a light upon it, the flame of which extended upwards into an angelic form in the colours of citrine, olive, russet and black. All these colours and shapes are in line with the conventional correspondences within the Golden Dawn system of the sphere of Malkuth.

Upon the eastern side of the temple three doors are to be seen, although it is only the central one that concerns us, which is veiled by a curtain upon which is depicted the Tarot Trump of the World – that is to say a great oval wreath of laurels intertwined with lilies and roses, about which are the four conventional figures of a bull, a lion, a man and an eagle, whilst within the dark oval within the wreath a pale naked hermaphroditic figure is seen to be approaching from a great distance, holding two spirals, one in each hand, of silver and of gold. The figure beckons and we visualise ourselves passing in through the wreath, into the picture.

The visualisation becomes three dimensional as we find ourselves seeming to be floating in a deep indigo mist that has the feeling as if it might be the bottom of an ocean, and so we begin to feel sand beneath our feet, with rocky and uneven surfaces, dark slippery weed, and various fish like creatures swimming round about us.

As we proceed on through this the way before us seems to get a little lighter and we see that there is a giant figure approaching us. He appears to be lame and has a large staff which he is using as a kind of crutch. He is about six or seven feet tall and seemingly Greek, and thus might be Oedipus – he who answered the riddle of the sphinx – or possibly the healing god Asculepius.

He is waiting for us, and as we approach looks at us searchingly and turns, limping off before us as our guide. The way we are going now seems to be more of a defined path until we come to what might be called a glade on the sea bed, although in place of trees there are great walls of weed trailing upwards, dark shadows all around, but in the centre, above us shining in golden light, the Hebrew letter of the Path, Tau, and the club footed shape of one of the two down strokes of this letter bears a certain resonance with the great limping figure who is custodian of this glade.

We pass on, however, and as we go we begin to feel that we are losing our weight, are becoming less dense and beginning to float upwards, and as we do so the dark indigo sea begins to become a brighter, almost Mediterranean blue, and we find we are about to break the surface of the ocean. As we do so, we find ourselves above the surface of the sea and in the sky, huge above us, is a close up view of the planet Saturn with its disc shaped rings and several moons.

Looking down from it we see before us a long low black barge – one imagines somewhat like the legendary barge which came to take the wounded King Arthur off to Avalon. There is a great tall figure within the boat, robed in purple, and, strange as it may seem in a deep sea, holding a long pole by which he is punting us along over the still surface of the sea beneath a starry sky in which the great planetary figure of Saturn is most prominent. We find we are approaching an island.

The island is of a grey kind of volcanic rock, and dominating it is a building of nine sides. As we watch, the building and the whole island begins to glow and to become translucent so that we can see through and inside it. Within we can see, seated upon a throne a great female figure, of heavy and ponderous build and white pallor of skin, surrounded by maidens, who appears to be a goddess of the Moon.

She holds up her hand in recognition and salutation to us and we remain contemplating this figure, to see if any realisations come to mind, be it in the form of words or pictures or ideas.

This is the further extent of our journey, towards the fringes of Yesod, and having gleaned what we can from this contact, we proceed in a reverse direction, following the association of ideas and images back to whence we came. Via the boat propelled by the tall figure, who we begin to associate with the archangel of Yesod and of Annunciation, the messenger angel Gabriel. Back to the point in the ocean where we broke the surface, down through the darkening waters to the glade containing the golden letter Tau, saluting the great lame figure as we pass, and thence back to and through the Tarot picture, through the wreath and into the visualised place from whence we started.

On a cursory reading this may not seem to have been a particularly significant experience, but it is another thing to proceed through the images slowly in a contemplative frame of mind, when the feeling will definitely be that, whilst it appeared to be just fanciful imaginings, yet somehow we have partaken of something real, that we feel we have 'been somewhere'.

This technique, that is known in some circles as 'initiated symbol projection' need not be confined to Qabalistic symbolism, but the Qabalistic system provides a comprehensive street map, so to speak, of the interior city of the soul, with its ten spheres and twenty two interconnecting paths.

Let us see how the same journey was undertaken by Charles Fielding. He begins with the impression that we are deep within the Earth, in a large cave with rock walls and beaten earth floor. The cave is in a rough cube shape and in the centre is a square cut granite altar upon which is an ancient stone lamp, whose light is reflected in the facets of a piece of rock crystal resting in an unglazed dish beside it.

At the eastern wall is a curiously carved ancient wooden throne behind which is a tapestry upon which is the life sized figure of a dancing woman, naked apart from a wind blown veil that covers her thighs, carrying two spiral rods, that twist in opposite directions, all within an oval wreath of laurel leaves. At the corners, as on the Tarot Trump of The World, are the heads of a man, an eagle, a lion and a bull. This picture has an ambience of great reality.

Then the light in the cavern grows brighter and the flame upon the altar grows in size surrounded by many motes of intense multi-coloured light. These are the 'souls of fire', inner energies behind the physical world, and as the flame rises up the roof of the cave disappears to reveal the night sky with the seven stars of the Great Bear prominent, and the flame itself seeming to make a kind of fusion with the pole star, Polaris. This heralds an awareness of an angelic presence, Sandalphon, the traditional archangel of Malkuth.

We then proceed to pass through the picture upon the eastern wall, which seems to be made of many lines of light something after the fashion of a television picture, and after a faint impression of passing through an archway, we find ourselves upon the other side, feeling more alive, lighter in body and clearer in mind, as if we have passed through some sieve or filter that prevents our grosser elements from coming with us.

The way ahead is dark but the way is illuminated to a certain extent by a faint greyish misty light emanated by our own bodies. A smooth rock path leads downward and becomes steeper, and rougher, even with dangerously loose scree. It also becomes narrower so that the indigo sky above becomes a mere narrow slit. Eventually the path flattens out and widens and gives onto a small plateau consisting of a sparse grove of ivy covered oak trees and a feeling of great age. In the centre is a tall single cypress tree, shining silver white in a light that shines down from directly above it.

Some vast silent presence begins to make itself felt as the spirit of this place. Past, present and future seem to coalesce as one, and we see the light above to emanate from a Hebrew letter Tau burning with a soft white radiance.

Moving on, the path leading on from the plateau slopes gently downwards and the sky above is once again filled with stars, until the path levels off and then gently rises towards a low ridge, its dark crest rimmed with faint silver light. Moving slowly up toward this crest we see for a moment a figure of the ancient god Saturn, looking rather like Old Father Time with his scythe, who vanishes however as we reach the top.

We find we are standing looking over a lake beyond the ground that falls away before us, and over a small rocky islet in the lake there hangs a crescent moon. Upon the island is a nine sided temple of Yesod seemingly made of crystal, shining with a violet radiance, encompassed by the aura of the great archangelic figure of Gabriel, whose wings fill the sky before us.

Having taken time to register this contact we then retrace our steps by the way we have come until we reach the place of our starting.

Turning to the similar journey undertaken by Dolores Ashcroft-Nowicki we commence in a somewhat more ornate version of the temple of Malkuth than hitherto.

It is once again square, with a black and white paving, and a stained glass window at each side representing a winged bull, winged lion, eagle and winged man or angel. In the centre is a black polished wood altar in the form of a double cube (that is, its height twice the dimensions of its square top). Upon it is a light in a bowl of deep blue crystal, standing upon an altar cloth of linen scattered with ears of wheat.

There is also a pair of pillars, one of ebony and one of silver towards the east, before three ornate doors, before which there stands Sandalphon, a somewhat Dionysian figure in the appearance of a young man with dark curling hair twined with grapes and vine leaves, clad in robes of citrine, olive, russet and black. He draws a pentagram in the air before the central door, which transforms into a figure of the Tarot Trump of The World, a dancer hanging motionless within a wreath of leaves. As we pass through we find ourselves in a landscape with a forest upon the left and a cornfield scarlet with poppies on the right. Immediately before us a meadow leads down to a small river with flat stepping stones, upon the other side of which is a limestone cliff that towers upward, and from whose summit a waterfall tumbles into a deep pool at its base.

A sound of weeping is heard and we find ourselves approached by a group of mourning women who turn out to be the goddess Demeter and her acolytes, seeking her lost daughter who has been kidnapped by Hades, the Lord of the Underworld. As they pass on we approach the river and cross by the stepping stones. Upon the other side at the foot of the waterfall is an ancient yew tree half concealing a cave entrance into which we go.

It is cold and damp and dimly lit by a small lamp at the back and a voice speaks from the darkness asking our reason for entering. It is the dark robed figure of the goddess Hecate who upon being told of our mission to find Persephone's kingdom indicates a narrow tunnel at the back of the cave and tells us it leads to Hades and we can take it if we dare. She gives us the lamp, however, to help us on our way, and two silver coins.

The tunnel, which leads ever downwards, is dark, cold, damp and slippery, sometimes very low and sometimes very narrow, along a tortuous route through which the wind keeps up a moaning sound like a woman in pain, until we eventually arrive at a vast under-earth cavern. Through the middle runs a dark, swift, deep flowing river – the Styx – its waters forming a natural barrier between life and death.

A boat is tied to the bank and by it stands a tall, broad, heavily bearded figure clad only in leather kilt and broad belt with leather pouch, and sandals. It is Charon, the ferryman, and around him shadowy figures throng, bending and swaying as if pleading with him. He strides through the misty throng, makes them draw back, and ushers us into his boat, which he pushes out into the river. Having reached the other side we alight and give him one of our silver coins. He points towards great double gates in the darkness; in the middle of each one is the Hebrew letter Tau. The gates swing open and we pass into a great hall hung with sombre tapestries, at one end of which there sits Hades, the Lord of the Underworld, and at the other a veiled woman wearing a crown beneath her veil and carrying a silver reaping hook.

As we come before Hades a black hound rises from between his feet, with three heads, and growling. It is the dog Cerberus, who guards his dark master. Somewhat apprehensively we look toward the king, a man of great height and majestic bearing, with hair, eyes and beard as black as night, and a crown of jet.

But as he leans forward we detect a gleam of laughter in his eyes. And his Greek costume reveals the body of a young athlete, not an old man. He stands and leads us towards his consort at the other end of the chamber, Persephone, the Queen of the Dead. At our approach she raises her veil and we look into the laughing face of a young girl crowned with flowers. And we realise that to this place come all, in their time, for Hades and Persephone are also the Lord and Lady of Rebirth, our planetary parents from whom we receive our earthly bodies.

Hades takes us to stand before a mirror and draws back the tapestry that conceals it. The glass seems liquid and full of movement and within its depths we may see our real and primal spiritual self as it was before we took form and as it will be at the end of time.

This is the climax of our journey. When the curtain falls back over the mirror we find we are alone with Cerberus who waits to guide us through another door and onto a seashore beneath a night sky filled with stars. Above us the planet Saturn hangs low in the heavens, like a great jewel between its rings, and the Moon rises from the sea, with its light making a pathway to our feet, and stepping a little way along it we feel as if the sea is solid beneath our feet.

Within the orb of the Moon, resting upon the waters we can see shadowy figures moving until, stepping from its depths comes the Moon mother herself, robed in black and silver, with crescent horns in her hair, bringing the gift of life. She envelopes us in her arms and as she does so we feel the scent of all the earth is in her hair and her kiss breathes immortality into us. Then she moves back from us, and returning to the Moon sphere rises with it into the sky, as we return to the shore.

There we find Cerberus barking and playing and leaping alongside his master along the shore. They escort us back to the hall and up to the cavern where Charon waits. He rises and takes the second of our silver coins and gives us passage back over the Styx, from whence we retrace our steps on the road home. Leaving the cave of Hecate we find the earth full of night sounds and scents, and Demeter together with her daughter Persephone walking together in the moonlight, to the sound of their laughter in our ears.

These three samples of modern 'pathworking' from three modern practitioners indicate something of the possibilities, and the usefulness of having a formal structure within which to channel the intimations of vision. It would of course be possible to use other symbolic guides or devices, or none at all.

The poet William Blake might be said to have used very free guides to his own vision, although there is, as is evident upon study, a firm structure within it, albeit it a somewhat arbitrary one. Nonetheless the creative imagination when used for aspirational purposes does have its own internal structures, just as there is a common pattern to a great deal of myth and legend world wide – a form of mythopoeic wisdom or perennial philosophy.

John Bunyan, the self taught seventeenth century mystic, also had his own journey system, as displayed in *A Pilgrim's Progress*, although this is more tightly controlled, in the form of Christological allegory.

I have also used the system of Dante that he uses in the *Paradiso* of the *Divine Comedy* and a passage from the Earth via the heavens of the Moon, Mercury, Venus, Sun, Mars, Jupiter, Saturn, the Fixed Stars and the Primum Mobile are but another form of the Qabalistic sequence of Sephiroth: Malkuth, Yesod, Hod, Netzach, Tiphareth, Geburah, Chesed, Binah, Chokmah and Kether, with their interconnecting paths that form the downward-striking creative path of the Lightning Flash emanating like the Word from the mouth of God, or in an upward direction the slow ascent of Neschamah, the Serpent of Wisdom.

The beauty of the Qabalistic system of pathworking is, though, that as developed over the past hundred years or so, it has become a device that can be rationally comprehended and systematically used. We have simply given examples of the treading of one path; there are twenty-one more, leading to transcendent heights, and in its various applications, can form a methodology that extends all the way from psychological integration to spiritual revelation.

The Tarot:
Fourfold Mirror of the Universe

FIVE HUNDRED years ago, northern Italy was the centre of the Western world. Florence, Venice, Genoa, Milan, Siena, Modena, Mantua, Ferrara, were thriving city states in which the famous Renaissance princes flourished. They bustled with artistic creation, international business and politics.

In Florence a large and active merchant class put their city in a position of great influence throughout the whole of Europe, with wool, exported from England and woven into fine products in the city, and sumptuous silks. Florentine bankers with agents in all the major cities of Europe financed kings and princes. The prosperity and internal stability of the city in the time of Cosimo de Medici, who ruled from 1434 to 1464, made this a 'golden age'. Artistic creativity was encouraged, and produced many of the greatest works of all time. In this scene were to be found great artists like Allesandro Botticelli and his master Fra Lippo Lippi.

It was during this time and in this place that the Tarot first came into being.

It was a time when much of the Western world was in chaos. The Wars of the Roses had just broken out in England, with Lancastrian and Yorkist families in a dynastic battle that lasted until the coming of the Tudors. And at the further end of Europe, the Ottoman Turks were besieging Constantinople. They killed the Emperor, and took the city, and this marked the end of the ancient Byzantine empire, and indeed of the Middle Ages. Nothing was ever quite the same again. The Renaissance was upon us.

This was effected largely by the tragic fall of Byzantium, which helped to bring about the rediscovery of the glories of the ancient world. The desecration of the monasteries and great libraries by the invading Eastern hordes released priceless manuscripts from their hidden archives. And though many may have been lost, the Renaissance princes, with their questing minds, eagerly used their money and influence to buy these manuscripts and have them translated.

Thus, in Florence, was Marsilio Ficino employed. A priest, a scholar and a doctor, he worked for the great prince Cosimo de Medici. His first task was to translate the works of the great Greek philosophers of antiquity, starting with Aristotle and Plato. But great as these works are, he was diverted from this task for something considered even more important, a translation of some writings called the Hermetic Scripts.

These were believed to be the work of an Egyptian priest and sage called Hermes Trismegistus. They were in fact a collection of scripts, written down some time between 100 and 300 AD, that contained an ancient oral tradition of wisdom that stemmed from many sources; the followers of Pythagoras, the Indian gymnosophists, the Persian magi, Chaldean astrologers, and wisdom culled from the temples of ancient Egypt that were at that time still functioning.

Marsilio Ficino and his contemporaries were intrigued by these scripts. They assumed a new approach to the mind of man and its powers. These powers of the mind had been condemned by the medieval church as heretical, because they had become associated with wild and superstitious beliefs about magic and sorcery which were used to exploit and terrify the ignorant.

However, it became apparent to Marsilio Ficino and his friends that they need not be so associated. That there could be a responsible, good and wholesome approach to this ancient tradition. This led on to the study of Greek authors of the status of Iamblichus, Porphyry and Plotinus, exponents of the highest traditions of pagan spirituality.

This newly discovered wisdom also had a practical side. Today we might call it applied psychology. Ficino experimented with meditation upon pictures or images as an aid to his medical practice. To counter melancholy (which doctors today might diagnose as depression and dose with tranquillisers) he advocated the powers of the Sun and Jupiter and Venus, which he came to call 'the three Graces'.

One of the ways to attract these harmonising forces was to gaze on pictures of them. It is possible that some of the famous pictures of Botticelli were commissioned for exactly this purpose. For example, The Birth of Venus, Venus Overcoming Mars, or The Primavera, which has the Three Graces of classical antiquity as part of its composition.

It is in this intellectual climate that the Tarot first appears. The earliest versions were beautiful hand-painted works of art, encrusted with gold leaf. They would have been highly suitable objects for meditation to bring down the powers of the higher spheres, or, as modern man might prefer to say, to contact the deeper reaches of the human mind.

Whether we use a fifteenth century or a twentieth century theory to account for it, the fact remains that the images of the Tarot are extremely powerful. They exercise a great fascination and are popular to this day, over five hundred years since their first appearance.

Part of their original popularity was through their being linked with playing cards. These made their appearance in Europe a few decades earlier, probably from India, along the trade routes of Persia to Egypt, and thence by Venetian galleys to Italy.

Whether it was by accident or design, the association of the 22 Trump Card images, or Triumphs as they were originally called, with the four suits of the playing card pack, has deep implications. What would have struck the Renaissance Hermetic philosopher would have been that the four suits of the playing cards mirror the Four Elements of the ancient world, Earth, Air, Fire and Water.

This is not such crude early chemistry as may at first appear. The four Elements also appear in the make-up of the mind of man, and this has proved a useful analysis of the structure of the mind for latter day psychologists. C. G. Jung, for example, equates them with the functions of Intellect, Intuition, Feeling and Sensation. Indeed he has used this fourfold structure to bring healing through the contemplation of images that emerge from what he calls the unconscious mind. These lead to a balancing fourfold image of healing that he calls a *mandala*.

The fourfold structure of the playing card pack is an extended mandala – a healing figure of psychic balance. Add to this the 22 figures of the Tarot and we have a powerful tool indeed – an intriguing system of interlocking images that can reveal the inner workings of the mind and of the world as we perceive it.

All new endeavour has to fight free from previous prejudice, and these matters, along with the more physical science of Copernicus and Galileo a little later, were considered dangerous heresies.

As science struggled free from religious intolerance it became more materialistic. Firstly so as not to appear to be poaching on the church's ground (as Copernicus and Galileo were accused of doing), and secondly because a physical experiment can be incontrovertibly proven. However, over the past three hundred years or so it has begun to form a body of prejudiced belief of its own which gives scant countenance to those realms of human knowledge and experience that cannot be objectively tested.

The time has come when many seek for knowledge of the inner world of man and of the universe. They seek it as a personal right and responsibility and will not be browbeaten by any established assumptions, whether scientific or religious.

The men of the Renaissance knew this, when the modern world first emerged from the mists of the middle ages. And although much of what they knew has been discarded and forgotten, it is still there for us to recover. For this edifice of knowledge and learning is founded on universal inner principles that are valid for all times and seasons.

A major part of it is to be found in the Tarot. All we need is the faith in ourselves and the lack of prejudice to approach it in the right spirit. We may well be amazed at what we discover.

When a subject is ignored or rejected, whatever its intrinsic merit, it attracts about itself accretions and assumptions that are unworthy of it. Thus, in its early days as a game of cards, the Tarot became associated with gaming and was condemned by churchmen of the day. In fact we owe to a worthy Dominican of the late fifteenth century a sermon against gambling games that preserves our first record of the names and order of the Tarot Trumps.

After a further three hundred years, in the time of Napoleon, it came to the attention of professional fortune tellers, and so became closely associated with tea-leaf reading and other social diversions of the times, encouraged by the Empress Josephine and other celebrities of the French court.

Yet it also attracted the interest of more serious minded people, particularly in France. Here, however, it became the object of such enthusiasm for ancient things that all kinds of claims were made for its origins. Some considered it to have had its origin in rites of initiation in ancient Egyptian temples beneath the pyramids and the Sphinx. Others that it represented a secret lore of the gypsies, sometimes called the Bohemians.

It also received close attention in the withdrawn circles of mystical fraternities, along with their study of other types of traditional symbols.

However it is in the past four decades, since about 1970, that the Tarot has really come into its own and made its presence felt in many walks of modern life, and at the same time become the subject of serious historical research. Furthermore, its images are to be found turning up in films, plays, musical shows, advertising campaigns, shop window displays. It is plainly coming up strongly into the consciousness of modern man. And so does he have a need for it? And what does it have to say?

When I was engaged upon my first book in the early 1960s, a compendium of symbolism that included the Tarot, it was impossible to obtain a Tarot pack in London, except as an antiquarian collector's item. The same applied to any books on the subject. Since that time not only have packs become freely available, they have proliferated. One can buy several versions of the standard Marseilles designs, reproductions of the early hand-painted Visconti-Sforza images, and a host of modern interpretations.

The Tarot has also excited much establishment interest. In 1984 the Bibliothèque Nationale mounted a fabulous and comprehensive display in Paris. It amassed a complete range of packs from the original hand-painted gold leaf embossed aristocratic Renaissance sets, through the many printed packs, to a version painted by the surrealist painter Salvador Dali.

The time has come when the Tarot can no longer be regarded simply as a popular card game of Southern Europe, or part of a stock of evocative images for use by display designers. Nor can it remain the encloistered province of occult fraternities, nor yet dismissed as part of the modus operandi of professional fortune tellers. The Tarot is for all.

It requires no special clairvoyant gifts or other rare abilities to use it, simply a knack of using the creative imagination – which is the greatly underestimated common heritage of us all.

The Hermetic philosophers of the high Renaissance knew all about this, and although their practical techniques could not be handed down to us in the form of a card game, they have nevertheless been preserved in other writings. These are particularly to be found in works concerning memory systems – which again are a recovery of ancient psychological wisdom from the classical world.

At a period when reading and writing were uncommon, and paper expensive, orators remembered their speeches – and indeed many of them. They did this by a technique of imaginative visualisation. They saw themselves enter a building within the imagination, often a theatre, and saw the points they wished to remember as objects at various locations. Hence the origin of the oratorical expression "In the first place … in the second place …" and so on.

These principles are the key to a working knowledge of the relationships to be found within the images of the Tarot. They make familiarity with 156 different images (the 78 cards either upright or reversed), and their meanings, a simple accomplishment.

By these means the Tarot becomes a symbolic language by which one can communicate with a level of consciousness that is different from the everyday mode that is limited to interpreting the perceptions of the five physical senses. Thus the Tarot provides the key to a whole new range of human ability.

This is not fortune telling. It is not superstition. It is a way of evaluating the dynamics in any current situation, some of which may not be immediately available to the rational mind.

One can consult the Tarot as one would an old friend. One can then either take that advice or ignore it. However, as with the advice of any old friend, its value can only be discovered by experience. It is only by trying to work with the Tarot oneself, in good faith, that one will ever come by that experience.

In 1884 a mathematician, Dr Edwin Abbott, published a book

called *Flatland: a Romance of Many Dimensions*. At the time it did not attract much attention because it dealt with the possibility of a fourth dimension, and this seemed utter fantasy to materialistic preconceptions at the end of the 19th century. However this was before Einstein, Lorentz, Whitehead and other modern physicists demonstrated that at least four dimensions are necessary to account for the observed phenomena of nature.

But although the whole subject has appealed to the popular mind, a fourth dimension is exceedingly difficult to grasp without a profound knowledge of higher mathematics. Dr Abbott's book went some way to overcome this – and again by the evocation of images in the visual imagination.

Imagine a world he said, confined to a plane, a sheet of paper, its inhabitants aware of two dimensions only, completely oblivious of anything above or below the flat world in which they live. If a solid downward pointing cone, for example, were to pass through their plane world, it would appear first as a point, apparently appearing from nowhere, which would then transform into a circle, gradually growing bigger until suddenly it disappeared altogether. This would seem a miraculous and unexplainable phenomenon to the Flatlanders. Likewise, a solid sphere passing through their world would appear as a gradually growing and then gradually diminishing circle.

As observers of such a world, we from our third dimensional viewpoint above them, would be invisible to them, but looking down upon them, as if we were looking upon a map, we could see all that was happening in their world, and be able to foresee things which were not apparent to them. A similar situation could be envisaged in the case of a helicopter hovering over a complex of city streets through which two cars, going at speed, are going to crash at an intersection. Only the helicopter pilot can foresee the coming disaster because of his superior vantage point. If he could radio to either of the car drivers he could prevent the accident – assuming, of course, that the car drivers believed him! Or had their radios switched on!

The use of the Tarot is similar to this. We are seeking the view of the helicopter pilot. Whether we observe the advice we receive is up to us. Whether we even seek it is also up to us. But the analogy demonstrates that by seeking the help of the Tarot, or any other means of extrasensory perception, we are neither denying free will nor seeking knowledge of a predetermined future. That would be mere fortune telling. What we are doing is seeking another view. Or equipping ourselves with a well tuned mental radio.

We are masters of our own destiny – the agents of our own fate. Life responds to us in much the way that we approach it.

By intelligent use of a system of higher apprehension such as the Tarot, we can discover more about ourselves and our motivations and how these are reflected back to us in the circumstances of daily life. This equips us to meet the challenges of life more confidently and more surely. In ancient Greece there was a great oracle to be found at Delphi, where thousands made their pilgrimage to have their problems answered. Upon its portal was the fundamental answer to all these questions, and also a challenge: "Get to know yourself!"

The Tarot is a system and method whereby we can learn to know the inner springs within ourselves and the circumstances that arise to confront them in daily life. Thus it is truly a fourfold mirror of the Universe.

Two key images in the Tarot Trump sequence are the first Trump, nowadays usually called the Magician, and the un-numbered image called the Fool. Each in their way are wandering mendicants – but this conceals a deeper significance.

The Fool or Beggarman owns only that which he carries, just as we all come naked into the world and depart from it in the same manner.

The Magician, sometimes called the Juggler or Mountebank in former times, is a travelling showman. He has set out his stall to demonstrate his skills and wares.

Both these figures are in transit. They have their origin and their goal elsewhere. In this sense they are also figures of deep importance – messengers, prophets and teachers- bringing enlightenment and news of other realms of existence to the astonishment – and often suspicion and resentment – of those honest burghers who live out their lives within safe city walls.

In their ultimate religious sense they represent two poles of the spiritual life of the Renaissance period On the one hand the mendicant principles shown forth by the lowly birth and subsequent mission of Jesus. At the other the power through knowledge of the tradition of the ancient magi who followed a star.

Four particularly important images in the Trumps have shown considerable mobility over the years in their appearance in the sequence of Trumps. Three represent Cardinal Virtues (Fortitude or Strength, Justice and Temperance), the fourth the World itself. They are distinguished from other Trumps in the hand-painted Gringonneur Tarot (for long thought to be the oldest version extant and by some still thought to be so), by having angular halos around their heads.

They thus have a correspondence with the four suits. Fortitude or Strength (sometimes shown holding a sceptre as in Botticelli's version, or as a man with a club) corresponding to Wands; Justice corresponding to Swords; Temperance corresponding to Cups; and the World corresponding to Coins.

The world itself, the ultimate Trump in the sequence, is in itself a mandala, showing the fourfold pattern of lion, eagle, bull and angel. These figures have their ancient parallels in the Biblical Vision of Ezekiel and in new Testament traditions they represent the four Evangelists, Mark, John, Luke and Matthew.

They also have an ancient connection with the Fixed Signs of the zodiac, (Leo, Scorpio, Taurus and Aquarius), and their associated bright stars, the Four Watchers of the Heavens, Regulus, Antares, Aldebaran and Fomalhaut – each at almost exact right angles to each other in the heavens as seen from Earth.

The Four Suits are represented here by the Aces, of Wands, Swords, Cups and Coins. These are the original emblems preserved in the Tarot to this day in Italian based playing cards. Our own ordinary playing cards have adopted a later French adaptation, of Clubs, Spades, Hearts and Diamonds.

The fourfold division of the world is an ancient concept originally described as the four Elements of Fire, Air, Water and Earth and the corresponding humours of man, choleric, sanguine, lymphatic and phlegmatic. A parallel to this fourfold division has been adopted by the psychologist C.G. Jung in the four psychological functions of Intuition, Intellect, Feeling and Sensation.

However, this fourfold system is to be found in many psycho-spiritual traditions, from those of the American Indian to the Mahayana buddhists of Tibet.

A fourfold regular pattern is called by Jung a mandala – a direct translation of an oriental term for 'magic circle'.

To the Renaissance mind the suits are allocated to the various interests of men: organisational activity (Wands); justice and preservation of law (Swords); love, pleasure and social life (Cups); and business, finance and material well-being (Coins).

These are the four Trumps that represent the four principles of Power – the Pope and Popess, representing spiritual power, and the Emperor and Empress, representing temporal power, each in their male and female aspects.

Thus we have two fundamental principles of polarity portrayed. The polarity of spiritual and temporal; and the polarity of masculine and feminine.

The principle of polarity is found in many ancient systems of spiritual philosophy, as yin and yang, *ida* and *pingala*, and the two pillars of Solomon's temple. These two pillars can be seen represented behind the Pope – nowadays usually called Hierophant. And they are to be seen covered by a veil in the image of the Popess – usually called the High Priestess. This represents the veil between the outer and inner levels of perception and knowledge. If we choose not to pass through them, then our world is one that is dominated entirely by the temporal polarities of the physical world represented by the Emperor and Empress.

Four Trumps fall under the presidency of Justice, and the apparently malefic influence of the suit of Swords. These are the Devil and the Lightning Struck Tower – which was once often referred to as Hell's Gate, as found in many medieval miracle plays. Also Death and the Hanged Man, formerly known as the Traitor.

Although superstitious medieval man was often frightened of these principles, they do have their positive and instructive side. The Devil represents our own shadow side that we can escape from when we face up to it and realise what it is. (It is often 'projected' as pet hates onto others.) The Tower is also the channel of spiritual realisation – a 'bolt from the blue' that may be shocking but also bringing us enlightenment and transformation. Death signifies all radical change, endings and new beginnings. And the Hanged Man, besides suffering ignominious punishment, forms with his body a secret sign and is tranquil in his condition. Thus he can be one who is not merely a traitor (whose effigies were hung upside down in Renaissance times), but whose values are different and possibly superior to those whose assumptions he has offended.

These four Trumps represent conditions of life, and not unexpectedly have changed somewhat in their imagery or significance over the past few hundred years.

Now called the Hermit, the Chariot, the Lovers and the Wheel of Fortune, they were originally Father Time and three goddesses of Victory, Love and Fortune.

The lantern of the Hermit was once an hour glass, and like Time, he went slowly on crutches, yet also had wings. The figure in the Chariot was once Winged Victory, familiar to the classical worlds of Greece and Rome. The Lovers showed a procession of lovers overshadowed by Cupid, the son of Venus, goddess of Love. The Wheel originally had the figure of the goddess Fortuna, who turned it whilst four figures about its rim rose or fell, or were at the height or depths of their respective fortunes – one saying "I am going to rule"; one saying "I used to rule", another "I rule", and the last "I rule nothing". We do not have to be kings for this to be applicable to us; we all rule or aspire to rule something, however small, and have also passed our best or failed to succeed in other areas of life.

These four Trumps show four different worlds, into which the cosmos is divided, according to the principles of the perennial philosophy. These are first the Heavenly World, represented by the Angel announcing the Last Days of Creation. Next there is the celestial world of the stars. Then there comes the solar system ruled by the Sun. The lowest world is the sub-lunary sphere represented by the Moon.

This tiered universe was of fundamental importance to ancient philosophy and indeed still is, because they are valid areas of the inner worlds and the discoveries of physical science and astronomy have not invalidated them. We now know that the direction of these spiritual worlds is within rather than without – that we do not get to heaven by rising up into the air. Rather, "the kingdom of heaven is within us", which is a cosmic rather than a mere psychological statement. As William Blake said, the external world is but a mirror in which the whole panorama of the inner worlds of man is reflected.

Index

Index

CPSIA information can be obtained
at www.ICGtesting.com
Printed in the USA
LVHW040958120120
643232LV00003B/323/P

9 781908 011527